No More Paraffin-Oilers

Rattray Head

No More Paraffin-Oilers

Ian Cassells

Whittles Publishing

Typeset by
Whittles Publishing Services

Published by
Whittles Publishing,
Roseleigh House,
Latheronwheel,
Caithness, KW5 6DW,
Scotland, UK

ISBN 1-870325-23-0

Printed by J.W. Arrowsmith Ltd., Bristol

For Patricia

Cantick Head

Contents

Acknowledgements

Many of the photographs are accompanied by an acknowledgement to the owner and we appreciate being able to use these images. Of those without an acknowledgement, many have been supplied by the Northern Lighthouse Board and grateful thanks are due to the Board and in particular to Lorna Grieve for her cheerful help in searching for and supplying photographs.

Introduction

The expression 'Paraffin-Oiler' was the old nickname for a Scottish lightkeeper, or to be more specific, a man born into a lightkeeping family who followed in his father's, and often grandfather's, footsteps and became a lightkeeper himself.

In 1786 the Northern Lighthouse Board was formed with a mandate from the British parliament to construct, man and maintain four lighthouses to help guide shipping around the dangerous Scottish coasts. By 1958, with the construction of Strathy Point lighthouse, the last major manned station to be built by the Northern Lighthouse Board, the original four lighthouses had multiplied to a total of eighty-four manned installations around Scotland. On the Isle of Man, for which the Board was also responsible, there were a further eight, but my story concentrates solely on those in Scotland.

Two years after the inauguration of Strathy Point lighthouse by Senior Lighthouse Board Commissioner Sir Robert Maconochie, the 'murder case' lighthouse of Little Ross was demanned and made fully automatic. With the automation of Little Ross the Northern Lighthouse Board began a remorseless programme of demanning and automation which has continued without ceasing until its recent completion. The Scottish lightkeeper has become an extinct species – there are no more 'paraffin-oilers'.

As a serving lightkeeper myself, this book is my tribute and farewell to the lights and the men who have manned them since that day long ago in 1787, when ex-shipmaster James Park assumed duty at Kinnaird Head lighthouse thus becoming the Northern Lighthouse Board's very first lightkeeper. IN SALUTEUM OMNIUM.

Ian Cassells

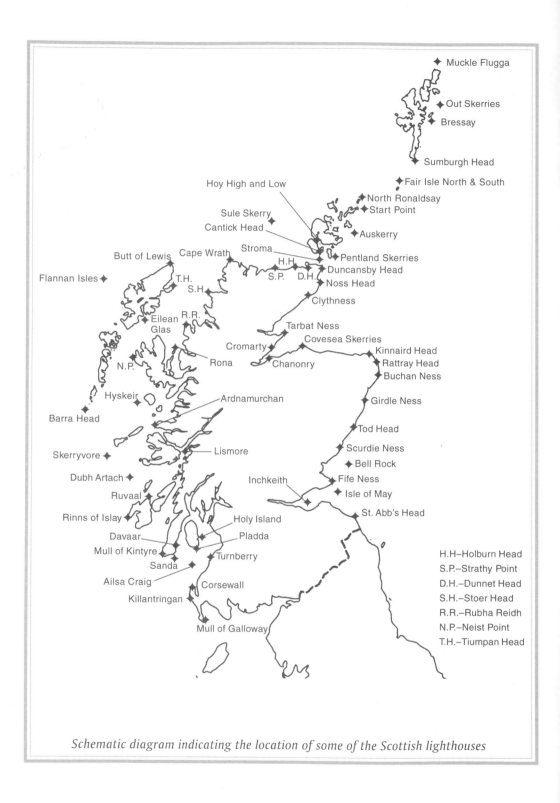

Schematic diagram indicating the location of some of the Scottish lighthouses

Muckle Flugga

Out Skerries

Bressay

Sumburgh Head

Fair Isle North & South

North Ronaldsay

Start Point

Auskerry

Hoy High and Low

Sule Skerry

Cantick Head

Pentland Skerries

Stroma

Butt of Lewis   Cape Wrath

H.H

Duncansby Head

Flannan Isles

T.H.

S.P.   D.H.

Noss Head

S.H.

Clythness

Eilean   R.R.

Glas

Tarbat Ness

Covesea Skerries

Cromarty   Kinnaird Head

N.P.   Rona   Chanonry   Rattray Head

Buchan Ness

Hyskeir   Ardnamurchan   Girdle Ness

Barra Head

Skerryvore   Lismore   Tod Head

Scurdie Ness

Dubh Artach   Bell Rock

Ruvaal   Inchkeith   Fife Ness

Rinns of Islay   Isle of May

Holy Island   St. Abb's Head

Davaar   Pladda

Mull of Kintyre

Sanda   Turnberry

Ailsa Craig

Killantringan   Corsewall

Mull of Galloway

H.H–Holburn Head

S.P.–Strathy Point

D.H.–Dunnet Head

S.H.–Stoer Head

R.R.–Rubha Reidh

N.P.–Neist Point

T.H.–Tiumpan Head

1

The Beginning of the Lighthouse Service

Officially it all started with 'Act 26 George 111 Cap. 101' dated 1786. This Act of Parliament authorised the erection of four lighthouses 'for the security of navigation and the fishermen in the northern parts of Great Britain'. In Edinburgh a Board of Commissioners was set up to implement the Act. This Board was composed of the Lord Advocate and the Solicitor General for Scotland; the Sheriffs of Edinburgh, Lanark, Renfrew, Bute, Argyll, Inverness, Ross, Orkney, Caithness and Aberdeen. The composition of the Commissioners has changed little over the past two hundred odd years, and is still principally made up of Scotland's senior lawmen, including both the Lord Advocate and Solicitor General for Scotland and no less than six Sheriff Principals.

Traditionally a number of the Commissioners (or 'Commissars', as one Principal lightkeeper I worked with would insist on calling them) would sail from Granton every summer on one of the lighthouse tenders, and then cruise around Scotland, following a fixed itinerary of lighthouses which were to be visited and inspected. I have noticed that about once every three years you can expect this manifestation at the lighthouse. For a couple of hours the place would swarm with a distinguished body of gentlemen, nattily attired in white peaked caps, navy blue blazers, fawn trousers and white pumps and exuding a faint aroma of expensive malt whisky! The venerable predecessors of today's Commissioners organised the first meeting of the Northern Lighthouse Board in Edinburgh on August 1st, 1786. At this meeting, John Gray, the Writer to the Signet who had drawn up the original founding Bill which had been presented to the Commons, and who came with the reputation of being 'famous for drinking punch, holding his tongue and doing jobs quietly', was appointed as first secretary to the newly formed Board. He was to remain in this job and carry it out with quiet efficiency until his retirement in 1811. Also appointed was an Edinburgh tin-plate worker called Thomas Smith who was selected to be the Board's first engineer, chiefly due to his experience in lamp making for the expanding new town of Edinburgh.

The Northern Lighthouse Board's first lighthouse was established on 1st December 1787 at Kinnaird Head near Fraserburgh. This was to be the first of many, resulting in a peak in 1958 of no less than eighty-four manned lighthouses around Scotland.

Principally because of the geographical situation of a particular lighthouse, and the number of men who were required to man it efficiently, the major lighthouses fell into different classifications. First there were those which could be termed 'shore lighthouse stations' which, as the name suggests, are situated around the rugged coast of mainland Scotland. At these lighthouses the lightkeepers lived with their families in dwelling houses at the lighthouse station itself. The men worked a staggered five day working week with normal annual holidays. A variation of these were those shore lighthouses which became one-man operated. At these, the sole lightkeeper needed keep no night watches and was little more than a caretaker. With exactly the same routine of work as that of a shore lighthouse station, and with the families also in residence, were the lighthouses classed as 'island family stations'. The only difference here is in the location, for, as the name implies, these lighthouses are situated on offshore islands. Next we come to the 'rock' and 'relieving' lighthouses; at both these types the total crew consisted of six men. These men worked a fixed routine of twenty-eight days on followed by twenty-eight days off, and at any one time three of the men would be on duty at the lighthouse while the others enjoyed their time off with their families at the shore station. The shore station could have been situated at some distance from the actual lighthouse itself. The relieving lighthouses are situated on the Scottish mainland or on the larger inhabited islands, but were considered to be in such a remote and inaccessible location that it would be unfair and impracticable to expect the lightkeepers' families to live there. However, this was not always the case. The 'rock' lighthouses are just what the name implies being offshore and situated on barren rocks, small uninhabited islands, reefs and skerries around the coast of Scotland. At these lighthouses the men worked the same routine as at a relieving station. Commuting back and forth to their work initially by boat, and latterly by helicopter, the 'rocks' formed the front line of lightkeeping.

Like their lighthouses, the lightkeepers themselves came under different classifications. A man would normally join the Northern Lighthouse Board's service as a Supernumerary Lightkeeper (S.L.K.). The earlier terminology for this rank was 'Expectant Lightkeeper' which in these days of equal opportunity could possibly have caused some embarrassment to lady lightkeepers! Basically a supernumerary lightkeeper was a probationer under training. He would travel from lighthouse to lighthouse, initially in the true capacity of his title as an extra man. Usually, as he gained more experience, he became a replacement for one of the established lightkeepers at a particular lighthouse who was temporarily off duty. During this time the Supernumerary would be learning the various aspects of the job, and a report on his progress would be sent to headquarters by the Principal lightkeeper of each of the lighthouses where he served.

When a man joined the ranks of the Supernumerary lightkeepers his name was arranged on a list in order of seniority. As time passed, and if he proved himself suitable, he would steadily climb to the top of this list. Once at the top, and as soon as a vacancy presented itself, he would be appointed an Assistant Lightkeeper (A.L.K.). He would then be permanently based at one particular lighthouse for a period averaging four to five years, before moving on. He would also then become eligible to receive the benefits which went with the lightkeeper's job i.e. rent-free accommodation for himself and his family and free fuel. A man normally remained a Supernumerary for about a year to eighteen months before being appointed as an Assistant lightkeeper. I spent thirteen months as a Supernumerary. Occasionally the Supernumerary at the top of the list would be passed over for some reason but this was a pretty rare occurrence. The initial year as a Supernumerary normally weeded out those who were not suitable for the job.

Once a man became an Assistant Lightkeeper he would find himself at the bottom of yet another list. As the long years rolled by he might reach the top of this list and discover that he had finally attained the exalted rank of Principal Lightkeeper (P.L.K.), also irreverently termed by some 'Pillock'! Now he would have a smart new cap badge, and one to wear on the sleeve of his uniform, and did not have to worry about being lighthouse cook any more!

The process of automation and the consequent shrinking of the service in recent years, meant that there were no Supernumeraries for some time. However, as automa-

Helicopter relief at the "Front Line" of lighthouses, Sule Skerry.

tion developed, a pool of lightkeepers whose own lighthouses had been demanned and automated were specifically employed as relieving lightkeepers. They took over the role of the Supernumeraries in providing cover for men who were off sick. There were two other ranks of lightkeepers employed by the Northern Lighthouse Board. The first of these was the Local Assistant Lightkeepers (L.A.L.K.) of which I was one. These men had exactly the same duties as Assistant lightkeepers but were never transferred from place to place, and were employed specifically to work permanently at the one lighthouse in their own locality. Local Assistant lightkeepers lived in their own accommodation and not a Lighthouse Board dwelling house, and did not qualify for the perks enjoyed by full Assistant lightkeepers.

Finally there were the Occasional Lightkeepers (O.L.K.) who were local men who worked part-time at shore lighthouse stations. They undertook watches at the lighthouse as and when required to allow the established lightkeepers to have some time off.

When looking back at a public relations handout issued by the Northern Lighthouse Board in March 1989, I smiled ruefully at the job description for the post of lightkeeper:

'Not every man is suitable to be a lightkeeper. The good lightkeeper has, or acquires the temperament necessary for this job which involves residence close to the sea and has much loneliness and isolation in its composition. While primary duty is to keep watch at night, to ensure that his light flashes correctly to character, and to keep a fog watch throughout each 24 hours, so as to be ready to operate the fog signal in the event of poor visibility, a lightkeeper must be a man of parts. He will acquire a good working knowledge of engines; at stations with Radio Beacons and Radar Beacons he will be initially responsible for their accurate operation; he will know about radio telephones; from his study of the sea he will respect its immense power; he will be a handyman of varying proficiency but mostly of a high standard; he will be a useful cook and a good companion. A lightkeeper will not make a fortune but he will be at peace with himself and the world'.

Hmmm ... well, I certainly agree with the 'will not make a fortune' bit!

Several people have asked me over the years how and why I became a lightkeeper. Well, as it now certain that nobody else will ever be taken on again in Scotland as a lightkeeper, I hope it is not too presumptuous of me to set down the story of how I personally got started. Even if my story is not exactly an archetypal example, it will nevertheless provide many comparisons with those of my contemporaries.

It all started in the winter of 1978/79. After nine years service I had left the Royal Navy (in which I had served as a signalman), and returned home to Caithness where I managed to find a job as a process operator with the Atomic Energy Authority at Dounreay. This was a job in which I was thoroughly bored and unhappy. To add to my problems at that time I was living in a severely dilapidated farm cottage some nine miles east of Thurso. The rent I paid for this hovel to the owner, a local farmer called Mackay, was one bottle of whisky a year. Mackay had refused to charge me a proper rent for the place for, as he quite rightly pointed out, if he did he would be legally bound to do something about the appalling state of the cottage. As in all things, the situation did have its bright side because Mackay would frequently summon me to the farm to receive a rent rebate. However, living conditions were deteriorating fast, and so was my liver, and I knew that I would have to make a move soon.

While sitting in the tea bar one bleak morning at Dounreay, one of my workmates pointed out an advert in the local paper which stated that the Northern Lighthouse Board was looking for men to work as lighthouse keepers. Amongst other details the advert added that it was a job which would suit men from a seafaring or rural background. My pal jokingly pointed out that since I was an ex-matelot living deep in the heart of the Caithness countryside, I was in danger of being overqualified! I was to find out later that by no means all lightkeepers are ex-seafarers. To give an example of a fairly typical cross-section of lightkeepers, and the past employment in which they were engaged, I will cite the examples of the crew I worked with at the Muckle Flugga lighthouse. Out of the six man total complement of the lighthouse, three of us were ex-seamen, one had been a labourer with Sutherland County Council, one a production-line worker at the ill-fated Linwood car factory and the last was a local crofter.

But back to that fateful advert. *Rent and fuel-free accommodation will be supplied to successful applicants on their appointment as an Assistant lightkeeper.* With my woeful domestic conditions in mind, this was the clincher, and for such prosaic reasons I decided to apply to become a lightkeeper. After an initial exchange of letters and once I had filled in an official application form, along with the names of two character referees, I was summoned for an interview with a personnel officer from the Northern Lighthouse Board to be held in the D.H.S.S. buildings in Wick, known locally as 'The Kremlin'. In the course of this interview I was given a questionnaire to fill in which included such questions as 'How would you change the washer on a leaky tap?' 'Fair enough', I thought, it would not be easy calling out a plumber to a small rock stuck in the Atlantic on a stormy night. But one question puzzled me then and still does now. It read 'What is a juggernaut?' Now I have always had an interest in foreign religions and myths, so I answered 'A juggernaut is an incarnation of the Hindu God Vishnu which was towed on a huge cart, and the faithful would often sacrifice themselves by throwing themselves under the cart wheels'. I handed over my paper which the personnel man quietly looked over until he came to the 'juggernaut' question. Giving me a long quizzical look he finally said: "Yes, you are quite right but 'a big lorry' would have done just as well."

The next part of the process was for me to undergo a medical by my family doctor. He gave me the once over, and a clean bill of health, and then asked me who would be paying for the medical, myself or the firm. 'The firm' I replied, buttoning up my shirt, 'why?' 'Oh good,' he said gleefully, 'I would not have the heart to charge you what I can charge them!'

A few more weeks passed and then I received word from the Northern Lighthouse Board to report to Edinburgh for yet another medical, this time to be carried out by the Board's own doctor. I do not believe that there were any specific criteria of health or physique which a prospective lightkeeper was required to possess. They obviously had to make sure that a man was fit enough to spend a period of four weeks in a situation where it may prove impossible to get him immediate medical aid, should some inherent malady suddenly strike him down. The Commissioners did once ask a Professor Madigan for advice on the health and physique of lightkeepers. This was way back in 1886 when a large number of cases of tuberculosis among lightkeepers was causing some concern. The professor recommended that the Board should only recruit men who reached the physical standards then required by the British army artillery regiments. He considered that a lightkeeper should be no shorter than five feet six inches in height, weigh at least ten stones and have a minimum chest girth of thirty-four inches.

I travelled down to Edinburgh and called in at the Lighthouse Board headquarters at 84, George Street. From here I was directed to the doctor's surgery which I found was situated in an elegant Georgian house in one of the quiet terraces which branch off the busy thoroughfare of George Street. Sir John Halliday-Combe (I hope I have got his name right) was the Board's doctor. His surgery was softly lit and reflected a quiet opulence of leather upholstery, polished hardwood and burnished brass ornaments. I wondered how the most outrageous charges my local doctor could make for medicals would compare with the fees likely to be exacted here! Sir John, a distinguished-looking gent in a dark conservative suit which gave him the appearance of one of the city's bankers rather than a medical man, bid me sit down and so began his examination. It did not get off to a good start. "Do you smoke?" enquired Sir John, "Yes," said I, "I do enjoy the occasional fag." "Hmm, I am the retiring president of ASH" came the slightly icy reply. (ASH stands for Action on Smoking and Health and they are the leading anti-smoking lobby.)

Despite this unpromising start, things began to progress pretty smoothly, especially when we mutually discovered that we had both spent some time out in the Far East, and a good ten minutes was spent in reminiscences about Singapore. Finally, the medical was completed and I was handed a sealed manila envelope, and with the parting words that I was A1 but should try and stop smoking! I headed back out into the bustle of George Street, bound for number 84, thinking to myself that it was the first time I had dropped my trousers in front of a Knight of the Realm!

More forms were signed at headquarters, and I had a brief introductory chat with the General Manager of the Northern Lighthouse Board, Commander John Mackay. I was then given directions to the Northern Lighthouse Board's tailors to be measured up for a uniform. The Northern Lighthouse Board is a uniformed service and quite a smart uniform it is too. It consists of a white peaked cap on which is worn a badge depicting a gold-coloured lighthouse with the letters 'N' and 'L' upon it. The uniform is a navy-blue reefing suit; the jacket has a shoulder flash on each sleeve bearing the words 'NORTHERN LIGHTHOUSES' in yellow, and is fastened by six brass buttons, each with a lighthouse and two buoys depicted upon them. These bear the words 'NORTHERN LIGHTHOUSE IN SALUTEUM OMNIUM', the Latin motto which translates as 'For the safety of all'. The Northern Lighthouse Board provides its keepers with new uniforms and working clothes on an annual points system.

NORTHERN LIGHTHOUSE BOARD

84 George Street, Edinburgh EH2 3DA

Telephone: 0131-473 3100

Fax No: 0131-220 2093

Operations Fax: 0131-220 0235

E-Mail: NLB@dial.pipex.com

The Northern Lighthouse Board's letterhead.

After I had been measured for my uniform I returned to headquarters at 84 George Street where I received my first posting as the Northern Lighthouse Board's newest Supernumerary Lightkeeper. I was instructed to make my way to Neist Point lighthouse on the Isle of Skye where I was to spend five weeks learning the basics of lightkeeping.

I was destined to spend just over a year as a Supernumerary Lightkeeper, in the course of which I worked at nine different lighthouses, visiting one, the Bell Rock, twice. I was eventually appointed as Assistant Lightkeeper on Muckle Flugga lighthouse in the far north of Shetland. After almost five years working at the 'Flugga', I was transferred to Stroma lighthouse in the Pentland Firth. For two years I worked there as an Assistant Lightkeeper and then the Local Assistant's job fell vacant. I applied for this and was successful. This was my job until the sad day when Stroma lighthouse was eventually demanned and automated.

The routine worked by lightkeepers at offshore lighthouses was pretty standard throughout the service. A twenty-four hour watch was kept, usually split between the three men into a four hours on, eight hours off system, with one eight-hour day watch put in to stagger the routine. It works out that you repeat your watches every third day. Day work such as cleaning and essential maintenance, was normally limited to between nine thirty and one o'clock, when dinner was served by the Assistant Lightkeeper whose turn it would be to cook that week. Afternoons were normally free time, but if there was any essential or urgent work to be done, this was undertaken after dinner. At one time all lightkeepers kept the watch in the lighthouse lightroom, but at the majority of lighthouses that became unnecessary as most of the essential equipment was then semi-automated and linked up to a noisy alarm system which alerted the lightkeeper on watch should anything be amiss. On watch, his main duties were to keep an eye on the visibility so that he would be instantly ready to start the fog signal should conditions deteriorate sufficiently to warrant it. If there was a radio beacon at the station he would have to check that this was transmitting correctly and at the right time, keep a general eye on the generator in service, and, most importantly, ensure that the main navigational light was working properly and flashing the correct character.

The earliest lighthouses displayed fixed lights, but as more and more lighthouses were constructed around Scotland's coasts it became apparent that some way would have to be found to distinguish each one. The distinguishing feature of each lighthouse is known as the lighthouse 'character'. This is not an aged lightkeeper with a fund of dubious stories, but the sequence in which the light flashes! For example, up here in the Pentland Firth where there is quite a concentration of lighthouses in a relatively small area, Stroma lighthouse has a character of two white flashes every twenty seconds. Nearby Swona lighthouse flashes white once every eight seconds; Cantick Head lighthouse directly across the Firth from Stroma has a character of one white flash every twenty seconds and finally, Duncansby Head close by on the Scottish mainland has a character of one white flash every twelve seconds. The officer on watch

The lens – this one is at Sule Skerry, taken in 1982.

on the bridge of a ship entering the eastern end of the Pentland Firth from the North Sea, has only to consult his Pilot book and stopwatch to know exactly which lighthouse is which.

The apparatus which revolved the light so as to display this precise character was principally a large clockwork machine driven by a carefully calibrated weight affixed to a light cable which ran down the centre of the lighthouse tower. When the weight reached the bottom of the tower the man on watch used to have to wind it manually back to the top. The time this weight took to descend to the point where it had to be wound up again, was called the 'Wind' by lightkeepers. Lightkeepers would comment that such and such a lighthouse had a 'wind' of twenty minutes, or whatever. I recall that the 'wind' at my first lighthouse of Neist Point was forty-five minutes. Of course, all of these manual winds have now been replaced by automatic winders, but when the lighthouses were still manned, it was the duty of the lightkeeper to ensure that the all-important character was correct at all times.

The most heinous crime in the lighthouse service was allowing a light to stand or show the incorrect character. The penalty for this was instant dismissal from the lighthouse service unless there were very real extenuating circumstances. A look through the lighthouse General Order book reveals a sorry catalogue of lightkeepers over the years who were given the sack for falling asleep on watch and allowing the light to stand.

Off-watch lightkeepers filled in their spare time in a vast variety of ways. Reading was probably the biggest favourite, and at some offshore lighthouses, such as Muckle Flugga when I was there, the local library would provide a box of books every three months or so. Weeks-old newspapers and magazines were avidly read, and it was greatly appreciated if anyone visiting a manned offshore lighthouse took the latest newspaper with them.

Back in the 1970s the Arbroath Fishermen's Association presented a colour television set to the Bell Rock lighthouse. This act of kindness and appreciation helped to embarrass the Board into providing all their other offshore lighthouses with colour television sets. Television is now the chief form of off-watch entertainment and at some lighthouses there are also video recorders. With three men there would be the inevitable differences of opinion as to which channel to watch, but things normally worked out quite amicably. Many lightkeepers had their own personal television set in their bedroom so they could watch what they wanted. In fact, at one time on Stroma, four of the six lightkeepers had their own television set in their bedroom. Come to think of it, I did not even have a television set in my home ashore at that time! When I was first at Muckle Flugga, the lighthouse was just out of television reception range. We did have a small portable black and white set which we could listen to while we watched the interference, if the mood took us, but truthfully television was not greatly missed. I used to listen to the radio a lot and my opposite watch were great card players, marathon sessions of canasta being very much in vogue. There was also a Monopoly set but Principal Lightkeeper Tommy Budge had to ban this game, after a heated argument arose during which one of the Assistants accused him and the other

Assistant of colluding against him and forcing him to mortgage his hotels on the lucrative Mayfair and Park Lane sites!

The usual hobbies, arts and crafts were carried out by keepers in their spare time. Woodwork was probably the most popular and I have seen some quite beautiful pieces of handiwork turned out. I can also think of three lightkeepers whom I have known over the years, whose artistic efforts with oil paints would stand up to inspection by the severest of art critics.

Outdoor pursuits normally fell into the three categories of fishing, creeling and gardening. All three were followed avidly on Stroma with varying success. One outdoor pursuit which often surprises people when they hear abut it, is that a number of lighthouse men were very keen on golf. This possibly came about because such lighthouses as Turnberry Point, Girdle Ness and Barns Ness are situated on or next to golf courses. However, the lightkeepers themselves constructed their own miniature golf courses at the lighthouses of Fair Isle South and Hyskeir, to name just the two that I can think of. I had an old set of clubs in my room on Stroma and occasionally I used to bash a ball about the island.

Although there is a great deal of bird life in the vicinity of most offshore lighthouses, I cannot really say that I met many keen ornithologists among my fellow lightkeepers. This does not mean to say that none exist, but just that I have not met any. I recall, when I was at Muckle Flugga lighthouse, that the nearby nature reserve of Hermaness was famous for its gannet colonies. On one occasion a black-browed albatross which had strayed severely off course, arrived in the north of Shetland where he decided to make his home with the gannets. This bird was quite famous and attracted twitchers from all parts of Britain, although I never actually saw it myself. A visiting Supernumerary, a young chap from Glasgow, quizzed me about the albatross which seemed to fascinate him. I replied that the best description I could give him was that it would look like a very big black-back (gull). He went outside to have a look around and had been gone for about five minutes when I heard him shouting to me to come quickly and see the 'albatross'. I rushed outside in time to hear him shout with amazement, 'Jesus! There goes another one, and look, another!' Aye, if you come from Govan, a gannet is a bit of a novelty!

Hopefully this chapter will have given the reader a bit of an insight into the life and work of lightkeepers prior to automation, and the setup of the Northern Lighthouse Board. In the rest of this book I will endeavour to take the reader on a tour of the entire Scottish seaboard where we will visit many lighthouses and I will tell you what I know about each one.

2

The Lights of Shetland

There is a particular place in the British Isles which is geographically farther north than Bergen in Norway, St. Petersburg in Russia, Greenland's Cape Farewell and even the Alaskan peninsular. Located in a position 60° 51.3' north, 0° 53' west, this most northerly outpost of Britain is little more than a barren, weather-beaten, waterless rock which rises to a height of two hundred feet out of the cold, grey northern ocean. On the windswept plateau at the summit of this rock is huddled a small group of white-washed buildings which, despite their height above sea-level, are frequently lashed by the huge waves whipped up by the cold winds blowing south from the nearest northerly landfall, the Arctic. Surprisingly, this isolated, inhospitable place used to be inhabited all year round. Two groups of three men would spend a month at a time living on this forbidding place. Twenty-eight days were spent away from their wives and families, seeing no other living creature but the countless sea birds and the nervous Atlantic grey seals which share the rock with them. The place is Muckle Flugga lighthouse and the men were the lightkeepers of the Northern Lighthouse Board who continuously manned and tended the light at this remote outpost for over 140 years until automation. The 'Flugga', as the place is familiarly, if not exactly affectionately called, seems to me to be an apt place to begin my farewell tour of Scotland's lighthouses, if for no other reason than that I was an Assistant lightkeeper there for five years.

The construction of a lighthouse in such a godforsaken spot as the Muckle Flugga came about as a direct result of the Crimean war. While the main theatre of operations in this conflict was obviously the Crimea, the Royal Navy expected to be involved in these waters as they carried out a blockade of Russia's northern ports. With this strategy in mind, the Lords of the Admiralty were only too well aware of a disaster earlier that century which had involved their Baltic fleet. A storm of near-hurricane proportions had suddenly sprung up and sunk the 98-gun First Rate *St. George,* along with the 74-gun *Defence* with the loss of two thousand men. The magnitude of this disaster can be fully understood when you realise that this tragic loss of life was more than double the number of Royal Navy seamen lost at the Battle of Trafalgar. The Navy obviously did not want a repeat of this catastrophe, and, on reviewing the situation, one of the obvious dangers was the unlit state of the dangerous north and east coasts of the Shetland Islands. The Admiralty immediately urged the government to rectify this situation by authorising the imminent construction of lighthouses on these treacherous, rock-bound coasts.

Anyone who takes the time to study in detail the history of the lighthouse service in Britain during the nineteenth century, will almost certainly be struck by the seemingly endless bickering between the Northern Lighthouse Board, the Elder Brethren of Trinity House and the Board of Trade, in a three-cornered fight over policy, lighthouse construction and, principally, finances. The events which led up to the eventual construction of Muckle Flugga lighthouse are a prime example. In March 1854 the Northern Lighthouse Board sent their engineer, David Stevenson, north to Shetland to find a suitable site for the northernmost of the proposed Shetland lighthouses. Sailing from the island of Unst, Stevenson had hoped to land on the skerry called Muckle Flugga which had been earmarked as a possible site for a lighthouse in a survey some four years previously. The weather was at its equinoctial worst and Stevenson was completely unable to land on the rock. In fact, he was so appalled by the conditions out at the Muckle Flugga, that when he returned to Edinburgh he flatly stated that in his opinion it would be completely impracticable to erect and maintain a light in such a place. There the matter rested until three months later when Trinity House decided to poke their oar in. A committee of Elder Brethren arrived on Unst on a fine calm midsummer day. They were rowed out to the Muckle Flugga on a sea like a mill pond, easily stepped ashore onto the rock and wondered what David Stevenson had been making such a fuss about.

A full-blown row between the two lighthouse authorities was narrowly averted when the wartime urgency of the situation was pointed out to them. After casting several aspersions about the Elder Brethren's 'fair-weather' visit, the Commissioners organised another survey of the site. This time, better weather allowed a landing on Muckle Flugga, and the Northern Lighthouse Board's engineers reluctantly conceded that the erecting and maintaining of a temporary light was probably practicable. Spurred on by the wartime priority of the job, once the Northern Lighthouse Board had decided to act they did so with impressive swiftness and efficiency. The lighthouse tender *Pharos* sailed from Glasgow on July 31st carrying aboard the materials for a temporary lighthouse, the dwelling houses for the lightkeepers who would man it and a squad of engineers to carry out the construction work.

A twenty-one foot high tower topped by a cast-iron lantern and temporary accommodation constructed of iron surrounded by a casing of rubble set in cement, were completed in time for the light to be exhibited for the first time on 11th October 1854. During that first winter, the lightkeepers on Muckle Flugga were almost to witness the complete justification of David Stevenson's initial misgivings about the siting of a lighthouse here. Although they were two hundred feet above sea level, at the height of the winter storms the sea broke against the structures of the temporary light and dwellings. The lightkeeper's kitchen was flooded with icy-cold sea water, the liv-

'While the buildings at Muckle Flugga could not be pronounced free from risk, that risk would not be greater or probably so great as would be incurred by shipping if the lighthouse were removed.' Photograph courtesy of Christopher Nicholson.

ing accommodation door was stove in, earth and stones were picked up and flung by the force of the wind against the lantern panes. Charles Barclay, the works foreman, had remained with the lightkeepers on Muckle Flugga to finish off the stairway cut into the rock leading up to the lighthouse from the boat landing. (His work is still there to be seen today with flat, hip-high stages cut into the side of the stairway at intervals, where a man could rest the sack he was carrying on his back.) During a lull in the weather, Barclay returned to Edinburgh with terrifying reports of sheets of white water regularly breaking over the summit of the Muckle Flugga, and the spray of this breaking against the buildings and rising to a height of over forty feet above the temporary light tower. Barclay was a man with much experience of working at exposed and remote lighthouses, and no alarmist. David Stevenson headed for London where he repeated Barclay's horror stories about conditions at the 'Flugga', and the future of the lighthouse was debated. Those concerned at the meeting came up with this eventual statement:

'While the buildings at Muckle Flugga could not be pronounced free from risk, that risk would not be greater or probably so great as would be incurred by shipping if the lighthouse were removed'.

Muckle Flugga lighthouse was here to stay.

Work on the construction of a permanent lighthouse at Muckle Flugga began in 1856. This lighthouse, designed by the Northern Lighthouse Board engineers, the brothers David and Thomas Stevenson, was to be an innovation in lighthouse construction as it was the first in such an exposed situation to be built entirely of brick. There were several advantages in using this particular kind of building material instead of the more usual heavy, pre-cut and dressed granite blocks. The chief of these was in the ease of handling which greatly speeded up the construction of the lighthouse. There is only one place where you can land safely by boat at the Muckle Flugga. This is in a narrow inlet formed between the bulk of the Muckle Flugga itself and a smaller stack called the Peedie Flugga. Even in this relatively sheltered spot, there is only a certain number of days in the year when a perfect landing can be made here by boat. With the decision to use brick for the lighthouse construction, the engineers found that the local boatmen could load up their small craft with a cargo of loose bricks, then, sailing out to the Muckle Flugga, would lie safely just off shore and throw their cargo out brick by brick to the workmen permanently living and working on the rock. Those Unst boatmen must have developed some powerful biceps by the time the 64 foot tower was completed and the light exhibited for the first time on New Year's Day, 1858.

A shore station for the Muckle Flugga lighthouse was built at Burra Firth on the north coast of Unst. A remote out of the way place for families to live, but it had some advantages. I used to tell my young daughter that she was a very lucky little girl because each Christmas when Santa came south from the North Pole, she was his very first stop in the whole of Britain! The Burra Firth shore station is now no more as the Lighthouse Board sold it off and at that time moved the Muckle Flugga lightkeepers and their families south. Also based at the Burra Firth shore station was the lighthouse-attending boat and boatman. The *Grace Darling*, named after a slightly better known lightkeeper's daughter than my lassie, was a large open craft similar to a ship's boat or lifeboat. It was powered by a Lister diesel engine and crewed by the permanent boatman with a part-time crew of six men to assist him. The crew of this boat were a living tribute to the hardiness of the Unst islander, as, excepting the boatman himself and one other, the remainder were all over seventy years of age! The bowman, Peedie Willie, was in his eighties and had worked on the Muckle Flugga boat since the 1920s. He also brewed the most potent 'home brew' I have ever tasted.

I recall one day being summoned over to the boat which was loaded up and ready to go at the small quayside at Burra Firth. Allie Sinclair, the boatman, asked if I would crank the engine for him as he had injured his back, and Tom Bruce, the other, younger man, was away for the day. With a dismissive gesture at the rest of his crew he commented: 'These old buggers just aren't fit for it!' I managed to get the engine started after a couple of turns, and, as I helped them to cast off, I commented to Allie about what they would do if the engine stalled when they were halfway out to the lighthouse. He gave me a long searching look then, with a shrug of his shoulders he said: 'Well man, we had better just row!'

With the advent of the helicopter, boats were no longer of the paramount importance which they once were at offshore lighthouses. Although the lighthouse relief was no longer carried out by the *Grace Darling,* water was still shipped out to the Muckle Flugga in large plastic barrels, as well as heavier stores, such as barrels of oil and the occasional visiting maintenance personnel. The barrels and stores would be winched up to the lighthouse by means of a 'Blondin' overhead cable, and personnel swung ashore onto the landing by derrick, while the boat would be held in position by a network of ropes in the inlet. They were ready at all times to cast off at a moment's notice should the seas in the inlet suddenly turn nasty, which they could do in the twinkling of an eye. I have been more than once at the Muckle Flugga landing, attending to the boat, when an unexpected and unheralded white roller has entered the mouth of the inlet and scoured the rock where I was standing, leaving me to hang on grimly to the guard rail as the freezing waters swirled around my waist. This happened if I was not quick enough to scramble clear up the metal derrick used for landing personnel from the boat. In such situations the boat crew could only sit tight and hope that their ropes held.

Life on the 'Flugga' was far from grim though. We had a pretty good crew, with one exception, but he was eventually moved on to plague somebody else. The lightkeepers would get up to all sorts of high jinks to break the monotony of the twenty-eight day tour of duty. I well recall the memorable 'prune-eating contest' which was held one summer evening, involving a couple of workmen who were out at the lighthouse at the time. But perhaps I had better gloss over this particular incident, after all this is not meant to be a horror story! There was also the dummy. I never really discovered where it actually came from, but a tailor's dummy appeared one day out at the lighthouse. Dressed in a lightkeeper's boiler suit and an old peaked cap, this dummy was the cause of all sorts of hilarity. It would appear on the lighthouse balcony – sitting atop the 'Blondin' mast. Once, it was carefully propped up against the guard rail by the winch house, while the attending boat was landing stores, and to our delight prompted the then boatman Lowry Edwards to shout in loud complaint from the boat below 'Is that lazy bugger not going to lend a hand?' But the dummy's finest hour happened during the annual visit of the District Technician and his engineers who were staying out on the Muckle Flugga whilst they carried out their annual maintenance. The engineers would invariably rise earlier in the morning than the night-watch lightkeepers and monopolise the one and only bathroom. The keeper up on watch one morning decided to do something about this situation and, after carefully removing the bathroom light bulb, he sat the dummy on the lavatory seat and then left the bathroom door a few inches ajar. When the other two lightkeepers arose for their breakfast they found those three engineers with towels draped around their necks and toilet bags in hand, standing in an impatient queue outside the bathroom muttering, 'My God! Is he going to be in there all day?'

I do not know what finally became of the dummy, he just quietly disappeared. Perhaps he went over the side and entertained the crew of some Norwegian lighthouse.

Muckle Flugga lighthouse has a character of two white flashes every twenty seconds. It no longer flashes a warning to the Royal Navy's Baltic Fleet, but stands as a warning beacon to the huge supertankers which pass en route for Sullom Voe.

When the Muckle Flugga's first temporary light went into operation in 1854, the lighthouse at the Out Skerries was also established at the insistence of the Admiralty. The 160 foot high tower of this lighthouse is situated on the Bound Skerry, the outermost of the small group of islands known as the Out Skerries, off the north-east tip of the fishing island of Whalsay and ten miles east of the Shetland mainland. There was a bit of a stir there during the Second World War when a crippled Norwegian motor torpedo boat drifted near the lighthouse and the crew, in their unfamiliar uniforms and with their foreign accents, were at first taken for invading Germans! This exposed and storm-lashed lighthouse, with its character of one white flash every twenty seconds, was demanned and fully automated in 1972.

Across on Shetland's western seaboard, the 37 foot high square, white-painted tower of Esha Ness lighthouse was constructed in 1929, in an attempt to warn shipping of the treacherous Ve Skerries situated eight and a half miles offshore. This did not prove to be completely suitable and in 1932 a buoy with a gas light on it was moored near the Ve Skerries, following the tragic loss, with all hands, of the Aberdeen trawler *Ben Doran*. Esha Ness, with its character of one white flash every twelve seconds, was demanned and automated in 1974, but with the steadily increasing volume of tanker traffic bound to and from Sullom Voe, it was decided to attempt to fix a permanent light on the Ve Skerries. A construction camp was set up at Esha Ness lighthouse station, and from here the helicopters shuffled back and forth with men and materials to the site of the new Ve Skerries light which was completed and exhibited for the first time in October 1979.

Esha Ness – constructed in 1929 to warn the unwary of Ve Skerries.

Guarding the approaches to busy Lerwick harbour is Bressay lighthouse established on the island of Bressay in 1858. An incident which occurred here some years ago illustrates just how conscientious a lightkeeper must be about his job at all times. It was a bright summer morning, the time of the year known in the Shetlands as the 'Midsummer Dim' when it never really becomes dark at all. The lightkeeper on watch that morning put out the light ten minutes before the official time, which would have been about four fifteen in the morning. A few days later he received a letter of severe reprimand from lighthouse headquarters in Edinburgh. Somebody across the water in Lerwick had been up and about at that time of day and had taken the trouble to inform headquarters that the Bressay light had been extinguished ten minutes early. Despite a gallant rearguard action by the Shetland Islands Council, Bressay lighthouse, with its character of two white flashes every thirty seconds, was demanned and automated in 1990.

Moving down to the southernmost tip of the Shetland mainland, where to seaward lies the turbulent stretch of water known as the 'Sumburgh Roost', and to landward, the bustling air terminal of Sumburgh airport, is the lighthouse of Sumburgh Head. This was the first lighthouse to be constructed on Shetland by the Northern Lighthouse Board. This lighthouse was built by the contractor John Reid of Peterhead back in 1821. Reid built the lighthouse walls of double thickness in an attempt to keep out the dampness to which a building on such an exposed headland would be prone.

I stayed at Sumburgh Head lighthouse briefly when I was a Supernumerary Lightkeeper en route to Fair Isle South, and found myself stormbound on the Shetland mainland. I was given accommodation in the lighthouse bothy where I met the Occasional lightkeeper, Andy, an elderly Shetlander of incomprehensible accent. Andy's hobby was carving models of old fishing boats such as 'Fifties' and 'Zulus'. He certainly had the knack of it and the examples of his work that I saw were true works of craftsmanship. As I spent a long wet afternoon in the bothy with him, I could not fail to notice that he had the unsettling habit of talking to himself as he whittled away at the hull of his latest creation. Well, he did not exactly talk to himself but rather addressed an imaginary audience to whom he would preach, scold, joke and berate, all in his broad Shetland tongue. I did hear more about old Andy sometime after I had been at Sumburgh Head. I happened to be chatting to another Supernumerary lightkeeper who told me that he had just spent a fortnight working at Sumburgh Head lighthouse, and had been staying in the new caravan there. I mentioned my surprise that they had a caravan at Sumburgh because the bothy had certainly been roomy and comfortable enough the night I had stayed there. 'Have they done away with the bothy?' I asked. 'No'. I was told that the bothy was not the problem but it was the old Occasional Lightkeeper the visiting Supernumeraries had to share it with when at the lighthouse for night watches. Apparently Andy had got into the habit of waking up the sleeping off-duty Supernumerary whenever he brewed himself a cup of tea during the night, and asking him if he would like a cup as well! Unfortunately, Andy was very fond of his tea! Sumburgh Head lighthouse, with its character of three white flashes every thirty seconds, was demanned and became fully automatic in the Spring of 1991.

Our final call in Shetland is the island of Fair Isle. This small remote island, world famous for its knitwear and a haven for ornithologists, boasts two lighthouses, both constructed in 1892. Fair Isle North lighthouse with a character of two white flashes every thirty seconds was demanned and made fully automatic in 1981. Fair Isle South was the last manned lighthouse in Scotland, 31st March 1998 marking the completion of the automation process.

When both these lighthouses were fully manned there used to be a keen inter-lighthouse rivalry between the two crews who used to play a monthly two-legged sports contest for the Fair Isle Lightkeeper's Trophy. A grand name for what was actually a cheap, plastic, silver-painted cup! The contest at the North light was a darts match which was followed a couple of days later by a golf tournament at the South light, where the lightkeepers had ingeniously constructed their own six-hole golf course using steamed pudding tins for the holes and broom handles, bedecked with red rags, for pin markers. I played a game on this course when I was a Supernumerary. Unfortunately the game was brought to a premature end when a particularly wayward swing by South Light Principal Lightkeeper Norrie Muir, hooked the one and only golf ball into the Atlantic! Golf and darts tournaments notwithstanding, both these lighthouses

Opposite:*Bressay lighthouse.*

have their place in Northern Lighthouse Board history. It was an incident at the North light which led to the introduction of automatic recorders being installed in lighthouse engine rooms to indicate an exact record of when the fog signal was in use. The Shetland mail steamer *St. Rognvald* struck the rocks off North Fair Isle lighthouse in thick fog. Onboard the steamer at the time was the Lighthouse Board's Superintendent Robert Muirhead. Several members of the crew of the *St. Rognvald* and Superintendent Muirhead claimed that they had not heard the North Fair Isle Light fog signal, but at the inquiry into the matter it was conclusively proved that the fog horn had indeed been blowing well before and after the stranding.

Fair Isle received a certain amount of unwelcome attention from enemy aircraft during World War Two, with both lighthouses coming under attack. During a raid in 1941 the outbuildings at the North Light were bombed and demolished by a direct hit. During the same raid at the South Light, the wife of Assistant Lightkeeper Sutherland was tragically killed by a bomb blast while standing by her kitchen window. Even worse was to follow six weeks later when the enemy aircraft returned in a concentrated attack on the South Light. In the course of the air raid a soldier manning a machine gun post at the lighthouse was killed, and a direct hit on the main block of the lightkeepers' dwelling houses claimed the lives of the wife and daughter of Principal Lightkeeper Smith. The lighthouse itself was also severely damaged. Out of this tragedy there came an act of gallantry and devotion to duty when Robert Macauley, one of the North lightkeepers, accompanied by his daughter, walked the three miles through snow drifts and gale-force winds to assist the badly-shaken South Light men to get their damaged light operational again before lighting up time that night. Macauley then walked all the way back again in the dark and snow to arrive in time to stand his watch that night at the North Light. Two water-filled bomb craters were still visible at the rear of the lighthouse station at Fair Isle South when I was last there. A grim reminder of that black day in 1942.

As I mentioned earlier, I worked for a time at Fair Isle South lighthouse when I was a Supernumerary Lightkeeper. One of the characters stationed at the lighthouse then was Assistant Lightkeeper Angus Edwards who hailed from Benbecula, or, as he would call the place, 'Benbecullar'. Angus had a wicked sense of humour, particularly at the expense of twitchers who visit Fair Isle in droves every year. His favourite ploy was to casually mention that he had seen a funny looking 'birdie' only that morning in such-and-such a location (usually an awkward to get to and out of the way spot). On being eagerly pressed to give a description of the bird he had seen, Angus would give a vague, but suitably recognisable to an expert, description of some rarity which he had earlier buffed-up on with the *Field Guide to Birds* he kept at the lighthouse. He all the time maintained, straight-faced, that he knew nothing about 'birdies' but had never seen one like this before! To Angus' great delight, an hour or so later, the almost

Opposite: Fair Isle South. 'Burn the damn tower to the ground...' Photograph courtesy of Christopher Nicholson.

inaccessible area in which he had claimed to have spotted the bird, would be swarming with eager twitchers, binoculars and expensive cameras to the fore, hopefully waiting to spot this once-in-a-lifetime rarity! His other favourite ploy was to wait until a sizeable number of birdwatchers had congregated on the foreshore by the lighthouse, a popular site for watching the sea birds. Angus would then quietly slip into the engine room and start the compressor for the fog-horn! I am surprised that they never had a couple of coronary cases on their hands after this particular antic, during which I personally witnessed startled birdwatchers jump several feet clear of the ground in reaction to the horn's loud blast! I chivvied Angus one day about his treatment of the twitchers, to which he replied that people whose only idea of fun was to spend hours gazing at some poor little 'birdie', obviously needed some excitement in their lives.

During my time there, Fair Isle South was one of the Northern Lighthouse Board's few remaining paraffin lights. The paraffin vapour light is similar in many ways to an overgrown Tilley lamp. Paraffin, usually stored in tanks at the base of the tower, is pumped up to an oil container in the lightroom which is topped up each morning by the man putting out the light. From here it is connected to an air pressure vessel which the keeper on watch pumps up occasionally during the night to maintain pressure. At the turn of a valve the paraffin is forced by air pressure into a vaporizer, and the resultant gas is burnt in a bunsen tube system which heats the lamp mantle to a high temperature causing it to glow incandescently; this in turn is magnified by the prisms and lens of the light. The cardinal rule you had to remember when lighting up a paraffin light was to heat up the vaporiser sufficiently with a small, methylated spirit-fuelled heater prior to the actual lighting up. If you failed to do this, or did not heat it sufficiently, then you could cause some quite impressive pyrotechnics! This is exactly what happened to me the first time I lit up at Fair Isle South. Fortunately, the display was more impressive than actually dangerous, and, on quickly switching off the vapour valve and then relighting, all was well. It did give me a bit of a start at the time though. I mentioned the incident to the Principal lightkeeper who was not overly-fond of being stationed at Fair Isle South, adding that I had thought for a moment that I was going to set fire to the tower. He gave me a bland look and quietly suggested that I light up again the following night, and possibly this time I might make a proper job of it and 'burn the damn tower to the ground and the rest of the bloody station with it!'

3

Orkney and the Pentland Firth

Looking southwesterly from the high balcony of Fair Isle South lighthouse on a clear night, you could easily see the measured ten second flashes of the lighthouse situated on the northernmost of the Orkney islands, North Ronaldsay. The 130 foot high red brick tower with its distinctive white painted bands, completely dominates this small, low-lying Orkney island famous for its seaweed-eating sheep. Although this high tower was constructed as long ago as 1854, the present lighthouse is not the original North Ronaldsay light. This is situated about a mile away on a spur of land called Dennis Head where stands the remains of the original, much smaller tower of North Ronaldsay lighthouse. This long-abandoned ruin is famous as one of the original four lighthouses first established by the Northern Lighthouse Board way back in 1789. Unfortunately this lighthouse had a relatively short and inglorious life. The first Principal Lightkeeper, a former master-mariner, was dismissed from the service for embezzling lighthouse stores. Then a spate of shipwrecks in the area caused the Commissioners to consider whether they had got things wrong and should re-site the light. They finally took action in 1809 and closed down the lighthouse at Dennis Head once a new lighthouse had been established at Start Point on the neighbouring island of Sanday.

The new Start Point lighthouse appeared to do the trick and the number of ship-wrecks in the vicinity fell dramatically, although this did not please everybody. Local fishermen and crofters were heard to mutter complaints about the poor pickings now being washed ashore from wrecked vessels since the lighthouse at Start Point had gone into operation. Start Point was the Northern Lighthouse Board's first lighthouse to have a revolving light installed. This lighthouse has a peculiar feature in the unusual style of paintwork on the tower, which is painted in black and white vertical stripes looking like a St. Mirren football jersey. Start Point lighthouse, with its character of two white flashes every twenty seconds, was demanned and fully automated in 1962.

The new lighthouse built on North Ronaldsay in 1854 had the distinction of being the last of the island family stations left in the lighthouse service. This fact did not make North Ronaldsay one of the most popular postings with many lightkeepers. This

Start Point – like a St Mirren footballer's jersey.

North Ronaldsay light in the distance with the original tower in the foreground.

Noup Head lighthouse, Westray.

island is quite possibly where the final chapter of the story of the manned lighthouses will be written. North Ronaldsay finally became the penultimate lighthouse to be automated when the lightkeepers were withdrawn on 30th March 1998, a mere 24 hours before the last demanning ceremony at Fair Isle South. However, other powers may not have been pleased with this change in plans as the final commissioning and testing of the new automatic light was delayed beyond that of Fair Isle South when the North Ronaldsay lighthouse received a major lightning strike on 21st June 1998. Before the lighthouses were established by the Northern Lighthouse Board, the eastern coast of Sanday and the island of North Ronaldsay held the dubious distinction of claiming more wrecks than any other islands in the Orkneys.

On the island of Westray, atop a rugged cliff face, which juts out into the stormy grey Atlantic sea, stands the only major lighthouse to be constructed on Orkney's western seaboard. Noup Head lighthouse, with a character of one white flash every thirty seconds, was established here in 1898 and was finally demanned and automated in 1964.

South of the island of Stronsay lies the small exposed island of Auskerry. In 1867 the Commissioners ordered the construction of a lighthouse here and, unusually for a

OPPOSITE: *Auskerry lighthouse, an early conscript into the forces of automation.*

small and remote island, Auskerry was conceived from the start as a family station. Communications between the lightkeepers and their families with the attending boatman, who was based on Stronsay, were carried out by a system of signals. This involved the prearranged positioning of round black discs on yardarms which jutted out from the sides of the lighthouse tower balcony. Some time ago I happened to be looking at a copy of the signals used at Auskerry lighthouse, and I mused upon the apprehension with which signal number ten, consisting of a single black disc on one yardarm, and two black discs on the other, would have been hoisted. This was the signal for 'Send midwife immediately'.

This simple system of visual signalling was used at a number of offshore lighthouses in pre-radio days. Of course, the principal drawback with such a method was that it was of absolutely no use in periods of poor visibility or bad weather. I also discovered that there was another unforeseen snag which once caused a bit of a panic at the Bell Rock lighthouse and the shore station at Arbroath. The lookout at the signal tower at Arbroath, where they used this system of signalling, spotted hoisted out at the Bell Rock lighthouse the code of two black discs on one yardarm which was the signal for 'Send boat'. A boat was duly dispatched from Arbroath and the lightkeepers families waited anxiously thinking that one of their menfolk had been injured out at

the lighthouse. Likewise the lightkeepers on the Bell Rock were equally puzzled and worried to see the boat heading out to them, and in turn they feared that something serious was wrong ashore. As soon as the boat was within hailing distance, the crew shouted out to ask why they had been sent for. The perplexed lightkeepers replied that they had certainly not sent for them. A short time later one of the lightkeepers managed to clear up the mystery. He recalled that earlier that afternoon he had seen two cormorants perched on the end of the signal yardarm, drying their outstretched wings. From a distance the lookout ashore must have mistaken these two 'scarfies' for a pair of black discs!

Auskerry lighthouse was one of the first to be dealt with when the automation programme started in earnest, being demanned and fully automated as early as 1961. The character of this lighthouse is one white flash every twenty seconds.

On the island of Graemsay, lying between the larger islands of Hoy and the Ork-

Hoy High (above) and Hoy Low (opposite) – sentinels on the Hoy Sound.

ney mainland, are the two lighthouses of Hoy High and Hoy Low. These twin lighthouses were established in 1851 to act as the leading lights for the narrow Hoy Sound and allow shipping safer access to the port of Stromness on mainland Orkney, and to the important naval anchorage of Scapa Flow. Graemsay man, Ronnie Mowat, who used to be the Occasional Lightkeeper at Hoy Low lighthouse, is in fact a descendant of the Irish works foreman who came to the island in 1851 with a squad of men and helped to build the two lighthouses. When the job was completed he married a local woman and settled in Orkney. Hoy Low was automated and demanned in 1966. Hoy High lingered on for twelve more years before going the same way in 1978.

East of Point of Ayre on the Orkney mainland lies the island of Copinsay with its adjacent stack called the Horse. A lighthouse was built here in 1915 due to the increase in Royal Navy shipping using the nearby anchorage of Scapa Flow during the First World War. Copinsay lighthouse was another of the Northern Lighthouse Board's

Copinsay lighthouse.

paraffin lights, and, in a more modern context, one of the first offshore installations to be used in trials of helicopters as a means of transport for lighthouse personnel. This took place back in the early 1970s. The tiny island of Copinsay is a nature reserve maintained by The Royal Society for the Protection of Birds. This led to a bit of friction with one of the Copinsay lightkeepers who was partial to duck eggs. His speciality used to be a five eider duck egg omelette. I would not have liked to have been left in a confined space with that chap once he had eaten his way through one of those! There is a tale about the Copinsay lightkeepers from the times long ago when a cart-horse was kept on the island to carry the heavier stores up from the landing. The lighthouse Superintendent visited the island, to be told by the three sorrowful lightkeepers that the poor old horse had finally laid down and died. The Superintendent was even shown a mound of freshly-turned earth which was where the tearful lightkeepers said they had buried the old horse. Before he left the lighthouse the Superintendent handed over an amount of money for the purchase of a new carthorse for the lighthouse, and then set off for Kirkwall and the boat south. Due to bad weather the boat's sailing was delayed and while he was waiting in Kirkwall, the Superintendent thought he was seeing things. There, coming down the main street was the 'dead' Copinsay lighthouse horse pulling an Orkney farmer's gig! The rogues on Copinsay had sold the horse to the farmer and then carefully prepared the 'grave' just before the

Superintendent's visit. It was just a combination of pure bad luck that caught them out with the farmer choosing the one day in months to be in Kirkwall in which the Superintendent was also stormbound in town. Be sure your sins will find you out!

Copinsay lighthouse, with its character of five white flashes every thirty seconds, was demanned and fully automated in 1990.

Now we come to the notorious Pentland Firth. These narrows between the northern Scottish mainland and the Orkney islands have some of the most fierce and treacherous tide-rips, eddies, overfalls and currents of any comparable stretch of water anywhere in the world. A vessel sailing with the tide may have as much as seven knots added to her speed. On the other hand I have watched some ships caught against the tide at its strongest, making virtually no headway at all but barely managing to keep position. Small wonder that back in the days of the sailing ships the narrow gap at the eastern end of the Firth was christened by the awed sailors 'Hell's Mouth'. Many skippers would take the far longer route around the top of the Orkney islands rather than hazard their vessels by sailing through the Firth. The Commissioners of the Northern Lighthouse Board were acutely aware of this dangerous stretch of water, and, as early as 1794, a lighthouse was established on the Pentland Skerries, a small group of islets, stacks and reefs in the very jaws of Hell's Mouth. The perils of the waters around the Pentland Skerries are clearly underlined by the impressive list of lightkeepers in that location who have been commended for their bravery in going to the assistance of mariners who have come to grief there over the years. To name some examples, back in 1871 it was reported that an Assistant Lightkeeper called Donald Montgomery dived into the seething waters and rescued a boy from the Wick fishing boat, the *Good Desire,* which had come a cropper on the Skerrics. Thirteen years later the whole lighthouse crew received a commendation for bravery when they rescued twelve men from the *Vicksburgh* of Leith, which had run ashore on the rocks.

In more recent years there have also been examples of heroism. In 1965, the 10,300 tonne *Kathe Niederkirchner* went ashore in the Skerries in thick fog. The two Assistant lightkeepers, Leslie and Macauley, shinned down the cliff and managed to get aboard the ship's lifeboat which was getting into difficulties. They took charge on board the boat and guided it safely to the lighthouse east landing where they safely put ashore the fifty crew and passengers. During the Second World War, as at the Fair Isle to the north, the Pentland Skerries received their fair share of unwelcome attention from Hitler's Luftwaffe. In the course of one raid, an enemy aircraft opened up with machine guns and strafed the light tower, scoring direct hits on the lantern and lightroom. The resultant damage amounted to eleven broken panes of glass and twelve damaged prisms; thirteen bullet holes were later counted in the copper dome of the light tower. A mere matter of seconds before the attack the entire lighthouse crew had been busily working in the lightroom.

On the lighter side of life, animals seem to have featured frequently in the history of the Pentland Skerries lighthouse. I read that back in the last century an enterprising Assistant Lightkeeper was fined by the Commissioners when they discovered that he was renting out part of the island to a mainland farmer for sheep grazing. A little later, after this incident, the Northern Lighthouse Board's records report a heated dispute between one of the Assistants and the Principal Lightkeeper which resulted in the Assistant writing a letter of complaint to headquarters. In it he accused the Principal Lightkeeper of 'maliciously causing the death of my cow'. I would dearly love to know what the full story behind this affair was. Still on the subject of animals, earlier this century the Pentland Skerries lighthouse was famous for a donkey which was employed there in those pre-tractor days, to carry stores from the boat landing to the lighthouse station itself. This animal apparently had the uncanny ability of knowing exactly when there was a boat due at the Skerries with stores, often before the keepers themselves knew about it. The wily donkey would take off and hide in the most inaccessible part of the island it could find, a couple of hours before the boat itself was due.

The Pentland Skerries lighthouse was a fully manned rock station with its shore station in Stromness. The character of the light exhibited here is three white flashes every thirty seconds. This lighthouse was demanned and automated on 31st March 1994.

A proud 200 years of heroism by keepers on the Skerries.

Duncansby Head. Photograph courtesy of Liam Whittles.

In sight of, and to the southwest of the Pentland Skerries, overlooking the mainland shore of the entrance to Hell's Mouth, is sited the squat square tower of Duncansby Head lighthouse atop the high headland of the same name and near the village and harbour of John O'Groats. This lighthouse was established here in 1924 on the site of a temporary fog signal, which had been erected during the First World War to warn the ships of the Royal Navy based at Scapa Flow of this dangerous headland. Duncansby Head lighthouse was, for many years, the radio control station for the offshore lighthouses of Stroma, Pentland Skerries, Copinsay and Sule Skerry. The keeper on watch at Duncansby would call up these lighthouses three times a day to check that all was well. This routine was discontinued in 1990, and at about the same time the fog signal at Duncansby Head was made redundant. Initially manned with a greatly reduced crew and almost completely automatic, Duncansby lighthouse was fully automated in March 1997.

In the middle of the Pentland Firth at its narrowest, is the aptly named island of Stroma. I say aptly named because the word 'Stroma' derives from the Vikings' name for this island – 'Straumey' – which translates as 'island in the stream'. Stroma lighthouse holds a special place in my affections as for seven years I was an Assistant Lightkeeper here, five as the Local Assistant. In fact, for a time my wife had this particular end of the Pentland Firth pretty well covered with family members. I was stationed on Stroma, her uncle was the Principal Lightkeeper on the Pentland Skerries, another uncle was the Local Assistant Lightkeeper at Duncansby Head and her brother Gordon was sailing back and forth past these lighthouses as the master of the short-lived Orkney ferry, *Varagen*. The lighthouse on Stroma is situated overlooking the dangerous tidal whirlpool called 'the Swelkie' at the extreme northern tip of the island. Originally, back in 1890, a minor light was established here by the Northern Lighthouse

Board. This was a highly unpredictable and combustible affair, fuelled by petroleum spirit which was kept regularly topped up by one of the islanders who was employed part-time by the Lighthouse Board. However, it was soon decided that Stroma was in too critical a position to be left as a minor light and in 1895 work commenced on the construction of a major manned lighthouse and fog horn. This work was completed, and the light displayed from the new lighthouse for the first time, in the following year of 1896. The importance of the nearby Flotta oil terminal probably ensured the survival of Stroma as a manned lighthouse for longer than might have been the case. However, Stroma lightkeepers were withdrawn on 21st March 1996. Yours truly then went off to the Job Centre to see if they had anything to offer an ex-lightkeeper with pretensions as an author! Extensive work was carried out in the automation of this important lighthouse. This included the removal of the fixed-beam system and its re-

Stroma – guardian of the Swelkie.

Cantick Head – a quiet night in the Firth.

placement with the ex-Sule Skerry lighthouse 4th-order lens which provides a range of 26 miles. This lens is rotated on a gearless pedestal powered by batteries which are sustained on a cycle charge system controlled by two air-cooled generators. The station is now monitored by radio link and PSTN with headquarters in Edinburgh.

Directly opposite Stroma lighthouse on the Orkney island of South Walls is situated the 68 foot high white tower of the lighthouse of Cantick Head established in 1858. This lighthouse, with its character of one white flash every twenty seconds, became an unmanned and automatic light early in 1991. Principal Lightkeeper Jimmy Budge was transferred across the Firth to become my boss on Stroma. Jimmy told me that the current of the Pentland Firth would rush so quickly past Cantick Head lighthouse that, at its full force, he had seen it bring to the surface a weighted lobster creel which he had hopefully cast off the rocks near the lighthouse.

Returning again to the Caithness shore, we come next to the lighthouse on the towering headland of Dunnet Head. The geographically minded will be interested to note that Dunnet Head is actually the most northerly point on the British mainland, and not John O'Groats where they have been happily conning the tourists for years with this particular claim to fame. The 60-foot high lighthouse tower and the flat-roofed block of the lightkeepers' dwelling houses were constructed on this windswept headland in 1831 by the contractor James Smith of Inverness. I recall visiting the light-house here as a boy with my parents, little dreaming that I would one day be working

Dunnet Head lighthouse.

at such a place. The Principal Lightkeeper who was there then was quite a character with some wonderful lines for the tourists who came to visit his lighthouse. I remember that we were up on the lighthouse balcony and I overheard him talking to some English tourists who were marvelling at the excellent view from this high point. 'Oh yes,' he said without batting an eyelid, 'on a clear day I have looked over to the west there and seen the *Queen Elizabeth* as she sailed from New York harbour.' I worked at Dunnet Head lighthouse for a short time when I was a Supernumerary Lightkeeper. It is a time which I chiefly remember because of a severe storm that struck the county, causing a power cut which blacked out the whole area including Dunnet Head lighthouse. The lighthouse was connected to the National Grid and had no emergency generator. I helped Assistant Lightkeeper Malcolm Williams to reconvert the electric light back to the old-fashioned paraffin apparatus which was still *in situ*, before the batteries powering the emergency light became exhausted. I recall musing ironically at the time on the ultra-modern technology just some thirty miles along the coast at Dounreay. Another problem caused by the power failure was the heating of the Local Assistant Lightkeeper's tropical fish tank, which he kept in the lighthouse bothy. I managed successfully to keep the fish alive by putting lemonade bottles full of hot water, boiled on a calor gas cooker, into the water of the fish tank. I was well-rewarded for this good deed. Some ten years later I married the tropical fish-fancier's niece.

With its measured character of four white flashes every thirty seconds, Dunnet Head lighthouse was demanned and became fully automatic in 1989. For a time the lightkeepers' dwelling houses were used as shore accommodation for some of the

Cape Wrath families, but this was discontinued in 1991.

Across on the opposite shore from Dunnet Head is situated the neat little lighthouse station of Holborn Head. When I was a young boy living in Thurso, many was the night when I lay in my bed listening to the regular whine of the Holborn Head fog signal, interspersed by the dull, distant boom of the fog horn at Dunnet Head. For better or worse, a foggy night here is si-

lent now as both these fog signals were discontinued a couple of years ago. With the increase in shipping calling in at the anchorage of Scrabster Roads, in connection with the then thriving Caithness flagstone industry, a lighthouse was first proposed for Holborn Head in 1853. Due to financial problems, the Northern Lighthouse Board would not establish a light here until nine years later in 1862. Holborn Head lighthouse was also attacked by enemy aircraft during the Second World War. Fortunately there were no casualties at the lighthouse although in the same raid, an armed trawler the *Beech* moored a couple of hundred yards away in Scrabster harbour, was sunk with all hands. In its later days the lighthouse became a one-man operation with the lightkeepers' dwelling

Holborn Head circa 1900 and, above, a more recent photograph.

houses being used as off-duty accommodation for the Stroma lightkeepers. I lived here myself for two years after I was first transferred to Stroma. Full automation came to Holborn Head lighthouse in 1987 with the retiral of the last Principal lightkeeper, Len Fraser, whose wife Kathy makes the best 'clootie dumpling' I have ever tasted! The dwelling houses here are now occupied by one of my fellow Stroma lightkeepers and two of the men from Cape Wrath. This fully automatic light has a character of a white/ red flash every ten seconds.

About twenty miles west of Holborn Head lighthouse, with the nuclear complex of Dounreay for its neighbour, is situated the square 35 foot high tower of Strathy Point lighthouse. In Northern Lighthouse Board history Strathy Point is a first and a last.

Strathy Point – the last major manned lighthouse station to be constructed in Scotland. Photograph courtesy of Christopher Nicholson.

Strathy Point lighthouse.

Although the erection of a lighthouse here was first proposed as early as 1900, it was not until as recently as 1958 when the lighthouse was finally established. This makes Strathy Point lighthouse the very last major manned lighthouse to be constructed by the Northern Lighthouse Board. The lighthouse also holds the claim to being the first all-electric station to be built by the Board. Due to this, Strathy Point heralded in part the eventual automation of lighthouses. It was made automatic in March 1997 and nightly displays a character of one white flash every twenty seconds.

Guarding the north-west approaches to the Pentland Firth we have to travel forty miles north of the Scottish mainland and a further thirty-two miles west of Orkney, to arrive at the low-lying thirty five acres of land which make up the island of Sule Skerry. Here is situated the remotest lighthouse in the entire British Isles. The 88 foot high tower and ancillary buildings took two years to construct, with the light exhibited here for the first time in 1895. As could be expected at a lighthouse in such a remote locality, Sule Skerry has had some highly imaginative and industrious characters work-ing there as lightkeepers over the years. One of the better known of these men was also one of the first, a man called John Tomison. Tomison wrote a series of nationally-acclaimed books on the island's bird life, and in those pre-radio days he carried out a series of experiments in communicating with the mainland by the use of a heliograph. Unfortunately these experiments were largely unsuccessful, and knowing from per-sonal experience just how little sunshine we see in the north some years, it hardly surprises me. Tomison would no doubt have been delighted to know that Sule Skerry was eventually to become one of the first lighthouses in Scotland to have radio communications installed. I was never at Sule Skerry lighthouse, although I did have a narrow escape when I was almost sent there as a Supernumerary Lightkeeper. Although relieved at the time, I now regret not having gone there. Over the years, I have known and worked with several lightkeepers who served their time at the 'Sule'. Whenever I have talked with them about the island, I have invariably noticed that at some point in the conversation they would all come up with the same comment about the place: 'Bloody puffins!' Apparently these cheeky-faced little auks at times inhabit the island so densely as to be almost of plague proportions. One ex-Sule Skerry lightkeeper told me that each morning his first job was to literally shovel out heaps of happy puffins from the warmth of the lighthouse engine room. The keepers were finally forced to erect fences to keep the inquisitive 'Tammy Noories' at bay. These fences were constructed out of chicken wire and the mesh had to be dug well into the ground at the base or else the industrious little birds would merely tunnel beneath them. In pre-helicopter days, Sule Skerry was notorious in the service for overdue reliefs. Once, the lightkeepers were stormbound on the island for over thirty-two days after the day on which their relief had been due. All in all, I am sure that there were more than a few sighs of relief when the last lightkeepers left Sule Skerry lighthouse in 1983. This lonely place is still visited by the Lighthouse Board technicians and, of course, there are always the puffins to keep an eye on things.

This brings us to the last of the Pentland Firth lighthouses. Standing on the top of the forbidding cliffs of Cape Wrath is the isolated 60 foot high tower of Cape Wrath lighthouse. Incidentally, the name 'Cape Wrath' has nothing to do with anger or fury but is a corruption of the old Norse word 'Hvarf' which means 'turning point'. This headland was where the Vikings of the old earldom of Orkney would turn their longships south when they were off to enjoy their summer holidays, raiding and pillaging among the Hebrides and Ireland.

Sule Skerry – 'Puffin Island'.

On a stormy October night in 1802, only two men survived out of the combined crews of three ships which were wrecked off the Cape, these tragic events thus initiating the campaign to have a lighthouse situated here. But it was to take twenty-six years before the demand was met and the Northern Lighthouse Board commissioned contractor John Gibb of Aberdeen to construct the lighthouse which was lit for the first time in 1828. A continual problem with the lighthouse at Cape Wrath is that it is situated on such a high headland that the light is often obscured by mist or low cloud. Just before the onset of the First World War, an ambitious plan was prepared to rectify this by building another lighthouse on the reef at the foot of the headland, and then connecting it to the existing one by means of a vertical shaft sunk through the cliff top. Work actually started on this scheme but was abandoned as impracticable and never recommenced after the first fifty feet of the shaft had been blasted out of the rock. Cape Wrath lighthouse has a character of four white flashes every thirty seconds.

Work commenced on its automation in the summer of 1997 with the landing at the station of 40 tonnes of building materials and the civil contractors to be involved in the job. Interestingly enough, a report in the Northern Lighthouse Board Journal stated that due to the large numbers of tourists who visit the Cape Wrath lighthouse, the contractor's first job was to make the area secure before automation work could begin. The work was completed by March 1998.

Cape Wrath lighthouse, taken from an old NLB Christmas greetings card.

Cape Wrath Light & Fog Signal & Radio Beacon Station
(most N.W. point of mainland of Scotland)

4

Hebrides and the North West – the Flannan Islands Mystery

Like an admonishing finger, the tall, red brick tower of the Butt of Lewis Light house has stood at the extreme northerly tip of the island of Lewis since it was first constructed in 1862. The Butt of Lewis lighthouse was one of the earliest in Scotland to have radio communications installed when the Commissioners reached an agreement in 1907 for the Marconi Company to install a wireless telegraphy system to be operated by the lightkeepers in order to supply news of shipping movements to Lloyds of London. The 'Butt' nightly displayed a character of a single white flash every five seconds and was automated by March 1998.

The Hebridean island of Lewis' only other major lighthouse station is situated at the tip of the Eye Peninsula near Stornoway. Tiumpan Head lighthouse was first established in 1900. For a number of years a fishery protection watch was kept here to keep an eye out for illegal trawlers. A new fog signal was fitted at the lighthouse which was first sounded by the then seven year old Prince Charles. Tiumpan Head has a character of two white flashes every thirty seconds, and was demanned and automated in 1987.

I would like to take a slight diversion from my farewell trip around Scotland's lighthouses, to say a few words about fog signals. Although they now seem to be going out of fashion, at one time the majority of lighthouses around the Scottish coast had a fog signal of some kind. Like the lights, the fog signals too had their own individual coded characters to distinguish one from another. These varied from the high-pitched, almost indignant wailing of the electrically-powered fog sirens to the deep, reverberating boom of the compressed-air-powered fog horns. I shall never forget my first experience of a lighthouse fog horn. I was at Neist Point lighthouse on the Isle of Skye where I had been sent on my first job as a Supernumerary Lightkeeper. It was towards the end of my very first week, and I was lying snugly tucked up in my bed in that half-conscious, dream-like state you fall into just prior to dropping off to sleep. Suddenly I shot bolt upright as the whole room was filled with a sound which I can only describe as resembling the deep, anguished roaring of some wounded sea monster. A thick sea mist had crept in across the Little Minch and the lightkeeper on watch had started the

The fog engine.

fog horn. Unfortunately for me this horn was situated directly outside my bedroom window! Once I had recovered from my initial shock – I bet there are still fingernail scratches in the ceiling of that bedroom – I rose and closed the heavy wooden shutters with which all lighthouse dwellings windows are fitted, to help muffle the penetrating noise. But even with the shutters tightly secured and a pillow over my head, I found it was still all in vain. You did not so much as hear the noise, but actually felt it jarring your very bones! It was a long, uncomfortable and virtually sleepless night.

Well, time passes and we get accustomed to most things, even fog horns. I was fortunate in my time at Muckle Flugga because there was not, nor ever had been, a fog horn at that lighthouse. There was an operational fog horn on Stroma, but I found that I became so inured to it that I normally just woke up at the first 'boom' when it initially started, and then drifted back off to sleep. I did, however, find one thing particularly annoying about the Stroma fog horn, and that was its uncanny ability of sounding off just when there was something you particularly wanted to hear on the television or radio. For example: 'We interrupt this programme to bring you an urgent News Flash … Booooooom!!' I have also found that the actual point when the visibility is considered sufficiently poor to merit starting the fog horn, is often a cause of debate among the lightkeepers. On Stroma, our guiding mark used to be the island of Swona opposite us on the Orkney side of the Firth. It was all quite simple; if I could not see Swona I would start the fog horn. However, Billy Gauld, one of the Principal lightkeepers who used to work with me on Stroma, would not consider starting the fog horn until the visibility had reduced to a halfway point between the two islands. He used to quite logically explain this by saying that if you were on a ship in the middle of the Firth in such conditions of visibility then you would clearly be able to see both islands, and besides, a ship would sail closer to us as there was no fog signal at the minor, automatic lighthouse of Swona. Yet another ex-Stroma lightkeeper did not believe in starting the horn until he could no longer see our hen house, about half a mile inland!

As with manned lighthouses, fog signals too are steadily being phased out of service. There has been a lot of debate about their value in this day and age, and when all the lighthouses in the Pentland Firth had operational fog horns, a day of fog could produce a truly confusing cacophony of sound as they all blasted out their own individual, coded character of timed hoots. As I mentioned earlier, Muckle Flugga never had a fog signal, and to the best of my knowledge no vessel ever came to grief there because of the lack of one. I have seen such thick fog at the 'Flugga' during the summer months that when I sent off the three-hourly weather report to the meteorological office in Lerwick, I was unable to give them the sea state simply because I could not see the sea! One thing is sure though, whatever happens there will be few lightkeepers who will miss fog horns.

But back to the lighthouses. This time we head out twenty-one miles northwest of Gallan Head on Lewis to the small, high-cliffed group of islands called the 'Seven Hunters', or, more commonly, the Flannan Islands. On the rocky thirty-eight acres of the largest island of the group, named without much imagination in the Gaelic, *Eilean Mor* (Big Island), stands the 70-foot high tower and ancillary buildings of the Flannan Islands lighthouse. Constructed in 1899 and after being operational for barely a year, this lighthouse was to earn a tragic place in the annals of sea mysteries with the disappearance, in December 1900, of the three lightkeepers, James Ducat, Thomas Marshall and Donald McArthur. Not long after the disaster the poet Wilfred Wilson Gibson wrote his famous poem *Flannan Isle*. It is a poem written with more than a certain amount of artistic licence regarding the facts of the matter, which triggered off in its turn, a whole catalogue of unsubstantiated and often outrageous theories as to the true fate of the three men. There is the long-time favourite tale of a curse on the island which transmogrified the lightkeepers into three black birds. Gibson was responsible for this one with his lines in the poem:

We saw three queer black ugly birds,
Too big by far in my belief,
For cormorant or shag

The prevalent fairy story these days is that they were abducted by a U.F.O. But is the Flannan Islands mystery really a great mystery at all? The events at the time of the discovery of the three missing men, and the subsequent investigation by Superintendent Robert Muirhead of the Northern Lighthouse Board, are well documented. From the evidence gained at the time, it is possible to come to a pretty sure conclusion as to

Flannen Islands Light, Hebrides Islands, Scotland.

A postcard of the Flannan Islands light.

what befell the three men, and to deduce within two hours the exact time at which they went missing. Here I will set down the known facts which I have gathered from the contemporary reports at the time, and which lay to rest some of the myths that have cropped up over the years. I will also give my comments, from the point of view of a serving lightkeeper, which even after the passage of time gives me a privileged insight into the likely events on that dark day in December 1900.

The first that the outside world knew about the tragedy at the Flannan Islands was a telegram sent to Edinburgh from Captain Harvey, the master of the lighthouse tender *Hesperus* which was dated December 26th, 1900. The telegram is reproduced here in its entirety:

'A dreadful accident has happened at the Flannans. The three keepers, Ducat, Marshall and the Occasional have disappeared from the island. On our arrival there this afternoon no sign of life was to be seen on the island. Fired a rocket but, as no response was made, managed to land Moore, who went up to the station but found no keepers there. The clocks were stopped and other signs indicated that the accident must have happened about a week ago. Poor fellows they must have been blown over the cliffs or drowned trying to secure a crate or something like that. Night coming on, we could not wait to make further investigations but will go off again tomorrow morning to try and learn something as to their fate. I have left Moore, Macdonald, Buoymaster

and two sea-men on the island to keep the light burning until you
make other arrangements. Will not return to Oban until I hear from
you. I have repeated this wire to Muirhead in case you are not at home.
I will remain at the telegraph office until it closes, if you wish to wire
me. Master, *Hesperus.'*

On 26th December 1900 the lighthouse tender *Hesperus* had come in to anchor in
the lee of Eilean Mor, carrying aboard Assistant Lightkeeper Joseph Moore who was
due to do his tour of duty at the Flannan Islands lighthouse. Normally, on sighting the
approach of the lighthouse tender, the lightkeepers up at the lighthouse would hoist
the ensign up the flagpole to acknowledge that they had seen the ship, and that there
was a safe landing for the ship's boat at the landing. If the landing was unworkable,
the blue and white chequered flag 'November' or 'Negative' would be hoisted. At first,
when there was no sign of any flag at all, no one on board the *Hesperus* would have
been too perturbed, and there would probably have been a few muttered comments
about 'the lazy beggars all being in their beds' or suchlike. So next the ship's siren was
sounded to attract the lightkeepers' attention. But still nothing stirred on the high-
cliffed island, and Captain Harvey, by now no doubt feeling the first twitches of un-
ease, ordered the firing of a rocket; but to no avail. Harvey then ordered that the
tender's boat be launched and Assistant Lightkeeper Joseph Moore should attempt to
land on the island and discover what was amiss. With a bit of difficulty Moore eventually managed to land on the island, and here in his own words is what he discovered.

'I went up, and on coming to the entrance gate I found it closed. I
made for the entrance door leading to the kitchen and store room, and
found it also closed and the door inside that, but the kitchen door
itself was open. On entering the kitchen I looked at the fireplace and
saw that the fire was not lighted for some days, I then entered the
rooms in succession, found the beds empty just as they left them in the
early morning. I did not take time to search further, for I only too well
knew that something serious had occurred. I darted out and made for
the landing'.

The badly-shaken Moore returned to the boat where he related what he had discovered to McCormack, the officer in charge of the boat. McCormack and a couple of
seamen returned to the lighthouse with Moore to see for themselves. They made a
thorough search of the lighthouse station, including the lightroom where everything
was discovered to be in proper order with the lamp cleaned, fuel fountain full and the
blinds, which prevented the sunlight shining through and being magnified by the lens
and thus possibly causing a fire, were down. After this second search proved unfruit-
ful, the men all returned to the boat and sailed back to the *Hesperus*. The first priority
now was that the light should be manned that night, and Captain Harvey ordered back

ashore Assistant lightkeeper Joe Moore in the company of the *Hesperus*' Buoymaster, a man called Macdonald, along with two seamen volunteers, Campbell and Lamont. These four men manned the lighthouse until assistance arrived. Captain Harvey then sailed to Breasclete on Lewis from where he sent his telegram.

At the Flannan Islands lighthouse the night passed uneventfully, and at first light in the morning the men organised a search of the island from top to bottom. Joe Moore reported the following details of what he found that day, and his comments on the matter, in a letter to the Northern Lighthouse Board dated 28th December 1900, which I largely reproduce here:

'The following day we traversed the island from end to end but still nothing to be seen to convince us how it happened. Nothing appears touched at the east landing to show that they were taken from there. Ropes are all in their respective places in the shelter, just as they were left after the relief on the 7th. On west side it is somewhat different. We had an old box halfway up the railway for holding west landing ropes and tackle, and it is gone. Some of the ropes it appears got washed out of it, they lie strewn on the rocks near the crane. The crane itself is safe. The iron railings along the passage connecting railway with footpath to landing are started from their foundation and broken in several places, also railings round crane and handrail for making mooring rope fast for boat, is entirely carried away. Now there is nothing to give us an indication that it was there the poor men lost their lives, only that Mr. Marshall has his seaboots and oilskins on, also Mr. Ducat has his seaboots on. He had no oilskin, only an old water-proof coat, and that is away. Donald McArthur has left his wearing-coat behind him which shows, as far as I know, that he went out in shirt sleeves. He never used any other coat on previous occasions, only the one I am referring to. From the monthly return it is evident they are missing since 15th. Up until 13th is marked in the book and 14th is marked on slate along with part of 15th. On 14th the prevailing state of the weather was westerly, strong breezes, showers. On 15th the hour of extinguishing was noted on slate along with barometer and thermometer inside and outside the lantern taken at 9 a.m. as usual, and direction of wind. The kitchen utensils were all very clean, which is a sign that it must be after dinner some time they left. There is one thing I know that Mr. Marshall never wore seaboots or oilskins only when in connection with landings.'

This letter from the first man on the scene debunks several of the myths which have grown up about the Flannan Islands lighthouse tragedy over the years. As a fellow lightkeeper I also find it possible to deduce a few facts from Moore's letter, particularly fixing to within two hours the probable time the men went missing. One major myth which is dispelled is the old favourite that the table in the lighthouse was set with a meal. The poet Gibson was again responsible for this with his lines in the poem 'Flannan Isle' which reads:

> *'We only saw a table spread,*
>
> *For dinner, meat and cheese and bread;*
>
> *But all untouched and no one there.'*

The 'abandoned meal' appears to have captured the imagination of commentators over the years. I have lost count of the number of so-called 'authoritative stories' about the Flannan Islands tragedy which concentrate on this imaginary dinner. The menu tends to vary as well from cold meat and pickles to meat and potatoes to plates of cold congealing broth with stale bread! But as we can clearly see from the letter, Moore states that the 'kitchen utensils were all very clean, which is a sign that it must be after dinner some time they left'. This statement in fact helps us to pinpoint the approximate time of the tragedy. At lighthouses then as today, the lightkeepers' main meal of the day is usually a good dinner which they sit down and eat at about one o'clock in the afternoon. After dinner the man who is cook for the week washes the dishes and cleans up the kitchen. Usually he finishes these tasks some time between one thirty and two o'clock. It is also known that the light was not exhibited that night of 15th December from a report which was received later from the master of the steamer *Archtor* (not the *Archer* which is wrongly stated in several accounts). Captain Holman of the *Archtor* reported, after news of the disaster became known, that he had sailed past the Flannans at midnight on the 15th and could not observe the light, although from the weather conditions and his position, he felt satisfied that he should have seen it. The light should have been exhibited that day at lighting up time which would have been at about twenty past three in the afternoon, at that time of year. The fact that it was exhibited on the previous night of the 14th is verified by the information on the slate in the lightroom, a job which the lightkeepers would have done during the fore-noon while the cook was preparing the day's dinner. We can therefore be almost cer-tain that the three lightkeepers at the Flannan Islands lighthouse disappeared some-time between one thirty and three twenty on the afternoon of Saturday 15th Decem-ber 1900. We shall now go on to consider how this might have happened.

On 29th December, lighthouse Superintendent Robert Muirhead landed on the Flannan Islands to carry out an official investigation for the Northern Lighthouse Board into the disappearance of the three lightkeepers. The following is quoted from the report he eventually wrote to the Board:

> 'On the Thursday and Friday the men made a thorough search over and
> round the island and I went over the ground with them on Saturday.
> Everything at the east landing place was in order and the ropes which
> had been coiled and stored there on completion of the relief on the 7th

December were all in their places, and the lighthouse buildings and everything at the station was in order. Owing to the amount of sea, I could not get down to the landing place, but I got down to the crane platform about 70 feet above the sea level. The crane originally erected on this platform was washed away during last winter, and the crane put up this summer was found to be unharmed, the jib lowered and secured to the rock, and the canvas covering the wire rope on the barrel securely lashed round it, and there was no evidence that the men had been doing anything at the crane. The mooring ropes, landing ropes, derrick landing ropes and crane handles, and also a wooden box in which they were kept and was secured in a crevice in the rocks 70 feet up the tramway from its terminus, and about 40 feet higher than the crane platform, or 110 feet in all above sea level, had been washed away, and the ropes were strewn in the crevices of the rocks near the crane platform and entangled among the crane legs, but they were all coded up, no single coil being found unfastened. The iron railings round the crane platform and from the terminus of the tramway to the concrete steps up from the west landing, were displaced and twisted. A large block of stone weighing upwards of 20 cwt, had been dislodged from its position higher up and carried down to and left on the concrete path leading from the terminus of the tramway to the top of the steps. A lifebuoy fastened to the railings along the path, to be used in case of emergency had disappeared, and I thought at first that it had been removed for the purpose of being used but, on examining the ropes by which it was fastened, I found that they had not been touched, and as pieces of canvas were adhering to the ropes, it was evident that the force of the sea pouring through the railings had, even at this great height (110 feet above sea level), torn the lifebuoy off the ropes.

When the accident occurred, Ducat was wearing seaboots and a waterproof, and Marshall sea boots and oilskins, and as Moore assures me that the men only wore these articles when going down to the landings, they must have intended, when they left the station, either to go down to the landing or the proximity of it. After a careful examination of the place, the railings, ropes etc. and weighing all the evidence which I could secure, I am of the opinion that the most likely explanation of the disappearance of the three men is that they had all gone down on the afternoon of Saturday 15th December to the proximity of the west landing, to secure the box with the mooring ropes etc., and that an unexpectedly large roller had come up on the island, and a large body of water going up higher than where they were and coming down upon them had swept them away with resistless force. I have considered and discussed the possibility of the men being blown away

49

by the wind, but, as the wind was westerly, I am of the opinion notwithstanding its great force, that the more probable explanation is that
they have been washed away as, had the wind caught them, it would
from its direction, have blown them up the island and I feel certain
they would have managed to throw themselves down before they had
reached the summit or brow of the island'.

I am in complete agreement with Superintendent Muirhead's conclusions about
the tragedy. Rogue waves over 110 feet high may be rare, but are not unknown. When
I worked at Muckle Flugga lighthouse, which has many similarities to the set up at the
Flannan Islands, particularly in being also exposed to the full brunt of the North Atlantic, we would quite often witness huge rollers appearing out of nowhere when weather
conditions at the Flugga did not seem to merit such waves. If the meteorological records
are checked, I am quite certain that they will report that there was a severe storm out
on the deeps of the Atlantic on 13th or 14th December 1900. The weather conditions
at the Flannans then had been blustery enough to suspect that this was the case.

I well remember one occasion when my friend and fellow Assistant lightkeeper
David Macdonald and I were working on the balcony of Muckle Flugga lighthouse. The
weather at the time was breezy, but far from gale force. The previous day we had been
hearing reports on the wireless about a severe storm out in the Atlantic and we had
been wondering if it was going to hit us. Suddenly David yelled a curse and grabbed
my shoulder, turning me round to see an enormous roller bearing down on the Muckle
Flugga, which crashed and broke with an almighty boom in the gully between us and
the adjacent Holm of Cliff Skerry. David and I were both drenched with spray, and you
must consider that at our position on the lighthouse balcony, we were a full 260 feet
above sea level! There was just that one rogue wave, no more, and the sea reverted
back to the merely choppy conditions which had prevailed before. Now if the two of
us, and the Principal lightkeeper had been working down on the lighthouse landing,
laying out new ropes or possibly carrying out repairs to the derrick, and that day the
weather would have been considered suitable for such work, I do not doubt that the
'Muckle Flugga Mystery' would have been speculated about for many years also!

Gibson helped further to foster the supernatural nonsense about the Flannan Islands
tragedy with his lines near the end of his poem which read:

    'We thought how ill change came to all
    Who kept the Flannan light,
    And how the rock had been the death
    Of many a likely lad -
    How six had come to a sudden end
    And three had gone stark mad,

High seas at Sule Skerry landing. If the two keepers had been manning the derrick when this picture was taken, this may have been another Flannan mystery.

And one, we'd all known as a friend

Had lept from the lantern one still night

And fallen dead by the lighthouse wall'

Victorian melodrama at its very best or worst! If this grim catalogue of disaster had been true it might possibly justify the years of speculation. However, at the time Ducat, Marshall and McArthur went missing the lighthouse had only been operational for just over a year, the light having been exhibited there for the first time on 7th December 1899.

A final few words about the Flannan Islands affair because it is a subject I feel quite deeply about, particularly as regards the more unsavoury theories which, although without any justification whatsoever, have reared their ugly heads over the past decade or so. For example, the theory that one of the lightkeepers was an alcoholic who dragged his companions over the cliff in a fit of the horrors. In similar vein, the story that one of the lightkeepers was a religious maniac who did away with himself and his two pals in a like manner. Most offensive of all is a play, produced by a so-called playwright, in which the three men kill each other as a result of a homosexual lovers' triangle which turned to violence. Amidst all this sensationalist speculation and downright fairy tales, it should not be forgotten that there lies a major human tragedy.

Three men in the prime of their life were killed while carrying out a job, the sole purpose of which is to help preserve the lives of others. Wives were suddenly left widowed and children fatherless, and even more poignant was the fact that all this happened at Christmas time. Moore was so badly shaken by what he had discovered that for the first couple of weeks at the lighthouse a seaman from the *Hesperus* was detailed to keep him company in the lightroom while he was on watch. In fact, Muirhead states in his report:

> 'If this nervousness does not leave Moore, he will require to be trans-
> ferred'.

William Ross, the first Assistant Lightkeeper at the Flannan Islands, was also troubled with a feeling of guilt that he had been on sick leave and Donald McArthur had only been at the lighthouse because of this. Finally Superintendent Robert Muirhead himself was badly affected as he had known the lost men well and had, in fact, personally selected them for the job at the new lighthouse. Only earlier that year, he had lived out at the lighthouse with them as the new station got over its teething troubles. The fact which particularly stuck in his mind was that he had been at the lighthouse as recently as the last relief day on 7th December, and, as he broodingly concluded in his report:

> '...and have the melancholy reflection that I was the last person to
> shake hands with them and bid them adieu'.

For seventy-one years after the disaster the Flannan Islands lighthouse remained manned without further incident. In 1971 the lighthouse was finally demanned and automated.

So we leave the Flannan Islands and their sad secret to resume our farewell tour of Scotland's lighthouses. We return to the mainland and the bleak, if ruggedly beautiful coast of Sutherland where we find sited the stubby, white-washed tower of Stoer Head lighthouse established in 1870. This isolated little lighthouse remained much of a quiet backwater over the years, being finally demanned and automated in 1978. Stoer Head has since found a new lease of life as the dwelling houses here have been retained by the Northern Lighthouse Board and are hired out as holiday homes to Board personnel.

Heading south along the rugged indented coast of the Scottish northwest mainland, we next come to the lighthouse of Rubh Re (Smooth Point). The 77-foot high white tower with a character of four white flashes every fifteen seconds, was constructed here in 1912 to mark the approaches to the deep natural harbour of Loch Ewe. This loch has long had connections with the Royal Navy, and during World War Two it was an important mustering point for wartime convoys. It was a vessel from one of these convoys, an American liberty ship called the *William H. Welch,* which ran ashore in nearby Black Bay on a dark and stormy night in 1944. Two Rubh Re lightkeepers

Stoer Head lighthouse.

received commendations for their actions that night. On foot, they covered a danger-ous expanse of snow-covered peat bog to reach the site of the wreck where they managed to assist in the rescue of fourteen survivors out of the ship's complement of seventy-four. Rubh Re lighthouse was demanned in July 1986, and I can recall exactly the day it happened. At the time I was involved in a solo marathon charity walk around all the manned lighthouses on the Scottish mainland. This walk was being done in celebration of the Northern Lighthouse Board's bicentenary, and to raise money for the Scottish branch of the R.N.L.I. After days of trudging through typical west coast summer weather (torrential rain!), I was looking forward to a dry overnight stay at Rubh Re lighthouse. With this thought uppermost in my mind I telephoned the light-house to inform the lightkeepers of my imminent arrival. A voice on the 'phone told me not to bother myself as there would be nobody there to greet me. They were officially demanned and all off home that very afternoon!

'If you can see Monach you are too near' was once a warning uttered by Hebridean seafarers. The Monach Islands are a group of four small islands some eight miles west of Baleshare in South Uist. According to legend, long ago the monks who then inhab-ited these islands used to display a light nightly to warn mariners. Monach lighthouse itself was established by the Northern Lighthouse Board on the outermost island of Shillay in 1864. The very first crew of lightkeepers to man Monach lighthouse earned a place in lighthouse history for their special devotion to duty when in that same year of 1864, the new apparatus for revolving the light broke down and Principal Lightkeeper Robert Seater with Assistant Lightkeeper Lauchlan Campbell, and an unnamed Occa-sional Lightkeeper, kept the light turning by hand for seventeen consecutive nights.

The lighthouse tender *Pharos* arrived at the Monachs with a new shaft, and while standing off the lighthouse the Captain timed the lightkeepers' manual efforts and praised them for keeping excellent time.

There was tragedy too at the Monach Islands lighthouse on 15th November 1936 when Principal Lightkeeper Milne and Assistant Lightkeeper Black took the lighthouse dinghy and set off across the Sound to collect overdue mail and provisions. On their return trip the already bad weather conditions deteriorated further and watchers on the shore soon realised that the dinghy was in obvious difficulties. A sudden squally blizzard of snow obliterated all view of the small craft, and when it cleared there was no trace of the two lightkeepers or their dinghy. Principal Lightkeeper Milne's sister was the only person left at Monach lighthouse. Miss Milne attended and stood by the light herself all that long sad night, until assistance reached her the following day. Tragedies involving small boats have had a long and unhappy history among lightkeepers. The year in which I joined the service four men were drowned in three separate incidents. In a severe gale the lightkeepers used to maintain that Monach lighthouse rattled like a 'speeding railway carriage'. During World War Two the lighthouse was first demanned and then discontinued altogether as an operational lighthouse in 1942.

Across the blue waters of the Little Minch, at the extreme western tip of the island of Skye, is the lighthouse of Neist Point, established in 1909. I have a particular regard for this lighthouse because it was here that I began my career with the Northern Lighthouse Board. I arrived as a very green Supernumerary Lightkeeper for a six week stay in which I slowly learned the rudiments of lightkeeping under the guidance of Principal Lightkeeper Donald Macleod. Apart from the obvious novelty of my new occupation, the chief memory I have of my time at Neist Point lighthouse was the excellent sea fishing to be had there. The lightkeepers had their own small boat and a ten minute trip out to a fishing mark in nearby Moonen Bay would almost always guarantee a box full of good quality cod, haddock and whiting after about an hour's fishing. On the shore, off the hexagonal basalt rocks at the foot of the lighthouse, you could catch coalfish, pollack and mackerel on little more than a bare hook. Shellfish were also fairly prolific in the waters around Neist Point and a couple of the lightkeepers supplemented their wages by creeling. One of the two Local Assistant lightkeepers was the most industrious and successful lobster fisherman at the lighthouse, when I was there, although during my stay he did experience something of a set-back. He had about twenty-five lobsters in a keepbox which was kept in the shallow waters near the boat landing, tethered to a ring bolt on the quayside. Without prior warning a southwesterly gale sprang up one night and smashed the keepbox open against the rocks thus liberating the lobsters. Now the keeper was in the habit of tying the lobsters' claws together with very distinctive, light blue elastic bands. To add insult to injury, about a week after his disaster with the keepbox, he received in the post a manila envelope which contained about a dozen of these light blue elastic bands together with a short note from some of the worthies in the local village of Glendale, thanking him for going to the trouble of securing the lobsters' claws before releasing them back into the sea for them to catch! When the local keeper received this letter and read its cheeky contents, I well recall that his language more than matched the colour of the elastic bands! Sadly there are no more lightkeepers to set a creel or haul on a hand-line at Neist Point lighthouse any more. This lighthouse, with its character of two white flashes every thirty seconds, was demanned and made fully automatic in 1989. The lightkeepers' dwelling houses were sold off by the Board a short time later.

In the middle of the channel between the island of Skye and the Scottish mainland, lies the island of Rona with its lighthouse established here in 1897. Before a lighthouse was built here a local widow called Janet Mackenzie used to display a light each night in the window of her croft house to warn local fishermen of the dangerous rocks at the harbour entrance. Janet Mackenzie was awarded a grant of twenty pounds by the Northern Lighthouse Board Commissioners in recognition of her good work. Rona lighthouse, or more correctly, South Rona lighthouse (so as not to confuse it with the other Hebridean island of Rona, a remote speck of land to the north of Lewis which also has an unmanned lighthouse station built in 1984), has a character of one white flash every twelve seconds. The lighthouse was completely demanned and automated in 1975.

At the narrowest part of this same seaway is situated the lighthouse at Kyleakin,

Rona lighthouse.

photographed by countless trippers every year as they pass by on the Skye ferry. Kyleakin lighthouse was established in 1857 to guide shipping through these narrow straits. The lighthouse was reduced to a one man operation as early as 1898 and was finally completely demanned in 1960.

Doubling back slightly northwards, we come to the island of Scalpay off the coast of North Harris. On Scalpay is situated the lighthouse of Eilean Glas historically famous as being one of the original four lighthouses first sanctioned and established by the Northern Lighthouse Board back in 1786. Eilean Glas was acquired by the Commissioners from Macleod of Harris, and the lighthouse was first lit in 1789. The first lightkeeper here was a man called Alexander Reid. Reid was paid the princely sum of £30 per annum, and received as perks a piece of garden ground, pasture for his cow and sufficient fuel for his family. Lightkeepers still receive this free fuel perk today. In years gone by, the principal lightkeeper on a small island such as Scalpay would be considered to be a man of consequence by the local community. He would be accorded by the local people the same sort of deference and respect as that shown to the laird, doctor or minister. Alexander Reid finally retired after thirty-four years at Eilean Glas lighthouse. On his retiral he was described in one contemporary account as being 'weather-beaten and stiff after so long an exposure at Eilean Glas'. Reid was the first lightkeeper here, and the last was Principal Len Fraser whom I mentioned earlier as being also the last to man the light at Holborn Head. Len left Eilean Glas when the station was demanned and automated in 1980, bringing to an end its 191 years as a manned lighthouse.

Just off the tail tip of the island of Barra is situated the southernmost of the islands of the Outer Hebrides, the small island of Berneray with its cliffs towering high above the Atlantic. Flashing white every fifteen seconds during the hours of darkness is the light of the lighthouse of Barra Head, standing atop a 56 foot high tower constructed from granite quarried on the island in 1833. Situated at a height of 683 feet above sea level, Barra Head lighthouse became notorious in the lighthouse service as one of the most fogbound lights in Scotland. For many years Barra Head was classed as a family station but the often continuous days of mist and low cloud which obscured the lighthouse led to problems with the emergency visual signals not being seen by the lookout and boatman based at Castlebay on Barra. Chiefly because of this problem, Barra Head lighthouse was another of the first in Scotland to have radio installed. The lighthouse was finally demanned and automated in 1980.

Nine miles south west of Rum can be found the tiny island of Oigh-sgeir, usually more commonly known by its anglicised name of Hyskeir. At 120 feet, the light tower of Hyskeir lighthouse completely dominates this low-lying island, and was constructed, along with the ancillary buildings, on this exposed ten acres of basalt in 1904. I spent some time here when I was a Supernumerary Lightkeeper, time which I chiefly recall as being spent digging up half the island single-handed. This hard labour was carried out all because of the fog horn, which was situated at the opposite end of the island from the main lighthouse buildings and engine room, to which it was connected by an underground pipe, along which the compressed air which powered the horn flowed. This

Hyskeir – 'Beware of the goat'.

pipe had developed a leak and Yours Truly was given a pick and spade and told to trace it. As if the job wasn't bad enough already, there was another problem to contend with that rejoiced in the name of Maisie, a nanny goat of venerable years and with a malicious sense of humour. At one time many of the offshore lighthouses kept a goat or two to supply the lightkeepers with fresh milk. With the introduction of the helicopter and U.H.T. milk, these animals became redundant. Maisie may possibly have her own niche in lighthouse history as being the last of the lighthouse goats. It did not take me long to discover that Maisie was quick to deliver a none too-gentle bump to the buttocks should I bend down to remove a large stone from the excavations. She would then swiftly run off to just out of well-thrown rock range and emit an evil bleat of triumph! On other days she would be in a sweeter mood of cupboard love and continually hassle me by attempting to poke her hoary old muzzle into my trouser pocket to see if I had brought her any titbits from the kitchen. However, there was one part of the tiny island of Hyskeir which was strictly out of bounds to Maisie and this was the small vegetable garden which the lightkeepers cultivated. It was one of the most productive lighthouse gardens I have ever seen in all my career as a lightkeeper. Life would not have been worth living had you been the careless one who had left the gate open and allowed Maisie access to this goat's paradise of succulent carrots, beet-root, cabbages, cauliflower, broccoli, onions and sprouts. Maisie must be long dead and buried by now and the lightkeepers were withdrawn from Hyskeir in January 1997. The character of the new automatic light, I am informed, has been marginally changed with the three white flashes every 30 seconds being extended by 0.1 seconds in the automation process. I think it would take a very sharp-eyed, very pedantic ships officer with a very accurate chronometer to notice the difference. I am sure that Maisie would not have.

Due east of Hyskeir, on the most westerly point of the Scottish mainland, stands the unadorned red granite tower of Ardnamurchan Point lighthouse which was established in 1849. I also worked at this lighthouse for a spell during my time as a Supernumerary Lightkeeper. The principal thing I remember about the place was the headache I had in actually getting there. Due to some ill-conceived travel instructions which I received with my orders to proceed to Ardnamurchan lighthouse, I found myself stranded in Fort William having arrived in the town half an hour after the last and only bus to Kilchoan, on the Ardnamurchan peninsular, had departed. I hadn't sufficient money for overnight lodgings, and besides, I was expected at the lighthouse that night. I could see nothing for it but to try and thumb a lift. Things started promisingly and I quickly picked up a lift on the outskirts of Fort William which took me as far as the Corran Ferry which I boarded with a glad heart to cross Loch Linnhe, confident that I would as easily pick up a lift on the opposite shore. Oh how wrong I was! I was left standing forlornly at the side of the road for a full two hours with as many vehicles

Ardnamurchan Point lighthouse

passing me in that time. Things were beginning to look as black as the dark storm clouds which I could see brooding over the hills. Suddenly the cavalry turned up in the shape of a battered grocery delivery van, and I was picked up for one of the most welcome and different lifts I have ever been given. I was taken on a mini tour of the West Highlands as the delivery van dropped off stores on its weekly supply route. Boxes of washing up liquid for a store in Inversand, cases of apples and oranges for Strontian and in Salen, we dropped off enough cat food to keep every moggie on the shores of Loch Sunart purring with contentment for days on end! After a delivery of tinned fruit and soft drink to the general store in Acharacle, we doubled back for the final stop in Kilchoan. Here I bid farewell to my Good Samaritan van driver and 'phoned up Principal Lightkeeper Jack Clark who arrived to collect and deliver me to Ardnamurchan lighthouse in time for my watch that night.

The next time I was to visit Ardnamurchan Point was during my walk around the Scottish mainland in 1986. My presence went pretty well unnoticed because the lightkeepers there at the time were busily preparing for the impending visit of a slightly better known personage, who was due to call in the following week. This was none other than H.M. Queen Elizabeth, as Ardnamurchan Point lighthouse had been the one chosen to receive the Royal visit in commemoration and recognition of the bicentenary of the Northern Lighthouse Board, celebrated that year. Two years after the Queen had climbed the spiral staircase to enjoy the view from the balcony of the red granite tower, Ardnamurchan Point lighthouse was automated and demanned.

To visit our next lighthouse we have to travel back offshore, and head ten miles west of the island of Tiree. Here, on a barren ragged rock, surrounded by treacherous reefs, is sited one of the masterpieces of Scottish lighthouse engineering, the Pillar Rock lighthouse of Skerryvore. Prior to the construction of a lighthouse on this exposed inhospitable spot, the site was visited by the Lighthouse Board engineer, Robert Stevenson in the company of the author, Sir Walter Scott, who was also a Commissioner. The place certainly left an impression on Sir Walter who was to write later: 'Skerryvore will be a most desolate spot for a lighthouse, the Bell Rock and Eddystone a joke to it'. Robert Stevenson's thirty year old son Alan was appointed as the engineer in charge of the construction of the lighthouse, and work commenced in 1838. Taking a tip from his father's construction of the Bell Rock lighthouse, Alan Stevenson first had constructed a sixty foot high barrack on the bare rock of Skerryvore. This barrack was to enable his workmen to work the maximum number of hours possible when they eventually began the construction of the lighthouse on the tidal rock. It took the whole of the working season of 1838 to complete this preliminary work, with the workmen and materials being ferried back and forth between Hynish on Tiree and the Skerryvore reef. With the onset of winter, and the barrack completed, Stevenson returned to Edinburgh satisfied with a job well done. A short time later he received a letter from his storeman at Hynish which contained the shattering sentence: 'Sorry to inform you that the barrack on Skerryvore rock has totally disappeared'. Alan Stevenson was shocked at this stunning blow, but he was not a man to be easily deterred, and when work commenced in the new season of 1839, an improved stronger barrack was

quickly erected a short distance from the mangled broken and twisted stanchions which was all that remained of the original one. This barrack survived the worst of the winter gales and work on the lighthouse began in earnest. On 7th July 1840, amidst great celebrations, the Duke of Argyll arrived at Skerryvore rock to lay the foundation stone of the new lighthouse. The brand new Northern Lighthouse Board tender, the paddle steamer *Skerryvore*, sailed out from the base at Hynish towing the lighters filled with the pre-cut and dressed stones which would make up the first courses of the tower. The first three courses were to be of Hynish gneiss, and the remainder of the tower would be constructed of granite quarried some thirty miles away at the Ross of Mull. Work proceeded smoothly and swiftly, and in July 1842 the last stone of the lighthouse parapet was finally laid in place. The elegant lighthouse tower now stood at a height of 137 feet 11 inches and consisted of 58,580 cubic feet of masonry which weighed something in the region of 4,308 tons. The lighthouse walls were nine and a half feet thick, gradually tapering to a thickness of two feet at the top. The interior of the tower measured twelve feet in diameter, and was divided into nine vertical compartments. The following eighteen months were spent on the construction of the lightroom and lantern and the fitting out of the bare tower. On 1st February 1844, less than six years since work first started on the original ill-fated barrack, the light at Skerryvore lighthouse was exhibited for the very first time. It had been a magnificent feat of engineering, but not without its critics.

The fact that a lighthouse was desperately required on this dangerous reef was not disputed. In fact in the fifty years immediately preceding the establishment of the lighthouse in 1844, no less than thirty-one vessels were known to have been wrecked on the Skerryvore reef and probably several more which had been merely listed as 'foundered at sea'. The criticism was directed at the cost of construction of the Skerryvore lighthouse, which amounted to the then not insignificant sum of £86,977 17s 7d. Many regarded this as unnecessarily extravagant, but then they possibly did not take into account that this cost also included the construction of a harbour, signal tower for communicating with the lighthouse and lightkeepers' dwelling houses, all based at Hynish on Tiree, and the construction of a pier on Mull. Time and tide have proved that the expense has been well justified as Skerryvore lighthouse has withstood the worst of the elements for nearly 150 years. In all that time there has been only one major interruption to the smooth running of the lighthouse, and that was caused by a different elemental hazard other than the usual ones of wind and wave, but one no less dangerous.

On the night of March 16th 1954, the lightkeeper on watch in the lightroom discovered that a fire had broken out in the tower in one of the compartments two floors below him. He immediately raced down the stairs and roused his companions, and together they desperately attempted to extinguish the flames. But the fire had by now got too strong a hold and was rapidly beginning to spread despite their efforts. The

OPPOSITE: *'Skerryvore will be a most desolate spot for a lighthouse, the Bell Rock and Eddystone a joke to it.'*

three men were forced to retreat further and further down the tower until they were finally driven out to take what scant refuge they could find on the bare rock of Skerryvore itself. Fortunately for the three lightkeepers, it was an unseasonably fair and calm night. But despite this blessing it must have been a nightmare for them as they huddled on the exposed rock at the mercy of a sudden change in the weather such as the blowing up of a March gale, and watched their only refuge become a blazing inferno occasionally emitting violent explosions as the fire detonated the fog signal charges. The weather held and so did their luck because the following morning was due to be the lighthouse relief day and the three men were quickly rescued from their ordeal by the arrival of the tender *Hesperus* shortly after dawn. Skerryvore lighthouse had been extensively damaged by the fire. Following an initial survey by the Lighthouse Board engineers, it did not take them very long to realise that it would be quite some time before things were back to normal. At first an unmanned lightship was moored nearby to mark the Skerryvore reef. A short time later an automatic Dalen light, a Swedish invention which was powered by acetylene, the containers of which were stored in the gutted tower, was put into operation. The repair work to the lighthouse, and the installation of a generator-powered electric light, took the engineers four years to complete, during which time the Dalen light worked smoothly and largely unattended. The reliable operation of this automatic light for such a long period of time convinced the Lighthouse Board technical staff of the feasibility of automating major offshore lighthouses. It therefore helped to initiate the programme of automation which has come to its inevitable and sad conclusion.

During the 1970s another major disaster at Skerryvore lighthouse was narrowly averted. A Bolkow helicopter was washed clean off the rock by an unexpected rogue wave. By sheer good fortune there was nobody on board the helicopter at the time, which was smashed and pounded on the reef. As a final postscript to Skerryvore's somewhat accident-prone record, a couple of years ago, Principal Lightkeeper Jimmy Burns fell off a vertical steel ladder at the lighthouse and shattered both his ankles! On 26th December 1991, Skerryvore's history as a manned lighthouse came to a close when Assistant Lightkeeper George Mackay came ashore to Oban for the last time. George had also been the final lightkeeper to man the last of Scotland's Pillar Rock lighthouses. Skerryvore would now wink out its warning of one white flash every ten seconds without the assistance of human beings.

There are only three Pillar Rock lighthouses around the coast of Scotland. This type of installation is an offshore lighthouse which consists solely of a tower, usually situated on a tidal rock, in which the men and machinery are all packed together in a strange, cramped vertical world. Skerryvore, which we have just visited, is one of the Pillar Rocks, and the most famous of them; the Bell Rock lighthouse, we shall come to later. The third, and possibly the least known of the three, is the last of our lighthouses of north-west Scotland, the Pillar Rock lighthouse of Dhub Artach. Situated on the dangerous Torran Reef off the Ross of Mull, the 117-foot high red-banded, grey tower of Dhub Artach lighthouse stands in solitary splendour on top of a storm-lashed 35 foot tall rock. Robert Louis Stevenson, author son of Northern Lighthouse Board

Skerryvore after the fire with the NLB tender Hesperus *standing by.*

engineer Thomas Stevenson, described this grim place beautifully: 'One oval nodule of black trap, sparsely bedabbled with an inconspicuous fungus and alive in every crevice with a dingy insect between a slater and a bug'. Little wonder that Robert Louis spent his latter days in the South Pacific! A base for the construction of Dhub Artach lighthouse was established at Earraid on the island of Mull. From here the pre-cut and dressed stones were shipped out to the construction site on the rock at the Torran Reef. As at Skerryvore and the Bell Rock before, a barrack was first constructed for the workmen on Dhub Artach. During the construction of the lighthouse Alan Brebner, the engineer on site, along with thirteen workmen, were marooned for five terrifying days in this barrack as a violent storm lashed the Torran Reef. At the height of the storm Brebner later reported that seas broke on the rock with such force that water fell onto the roof of the barrack, 77 feet above the high water mark. During yet another severe gale the rock was washed with waves of such a force that eleven two-ton, pre-cut stones were dislodged from their position in the course of the lighthouse and deposited in deep water. This same gale also severely damaged landing cranes and other apparatus, but fortunately once again there was no loss of life or serious

The building of Dhub Artach, 1871 and, below, Earraid, the construction base for Dhub Artach.

Earraid, the construction base for Dhub Artach.

Transportation of stone for the building of Dhub Artach.

injury. With the approach of better weather work was resumed and the tower was eventually completed and became fully operational in 1872, having cost £65,784 to complete. The very first Principal Lightkeeper at Dhub Artach lighthouse was James Ewing, a 'paraffin-oiler' whose father and grandfather before him were both lightkeepers. When Dhub Artach lighthouse was finally demanned and automated in 1971, many a lightkeeper breathed a sigh of relief that the 'Black Rock' would be one particular transfer that they would not have to worry about any more. In the pre-helicopter days the place was notorious for overdue reliefs, and I have heard several horror stories of the lightkeepers living off stale mouldy bread, soaked in water and re-baked in the oven, eaten with endless tins of corned beef. In fact, in January 1947 the relief went so long overdue that two light aircraft were hired to drop emergency food parcels to the marooned lightkeepers.

Merely getting on and off the rock at Dubh Artach was, in itself, an operation fraught with difficulty and danger. There was a height of forty feet between the landing and the deck of the ship's boat at low water. Personnel had to be swung onto the landing by derrick in even the calmest of weather. Yes indeed, this was at least one demanning and automation which was more than welcome!

The challenge of relief day at Dhub Artach (above) and January relief at the light (lower, opposite).

Not for the faint-hearted – relief day at Dhub Artach.

5

The Clyde Approaches and South West Scotland

Guiding shipping through the narrow Sound of Mull is the lighthouse of Rubha Nan Gall, constructed in 1857. This was reduced to a one man operated lighthouse as early as 1898, and was also one of the earliest to be dealt with in the Northern Lighthouse Board's automation programme, being completely demanned in 1960.

In the nearby Firth of Lorne on the small island of Eilean Musdile off the southern tip of Lismore, a splash of white appears in contrast to the dark hills. This is the tower and ancillary buildings of Lismore lighthouse which first emitted its single white flashes at ten second intervals, back in 1833. The lighthouse and buildings were constructed at this beautiful but lonely site by the Inverness contractor John Smith. In the mid-nineteenth century there was a certain amount of concern voiced regarding the spiritual welfare of the lightkeepers and their families stationed at Lismore lighthouse when it was discovered that the nearest parish church was an inaccessible twelve miles away. During the dark days of 1940, two Lismore lightkeepers, Principal Donald Macdonald and Assistant William Budge, were commended for their brave rescue of two downed airmen who were adrift in a stormy Firth of Lorne, clinging to the wreckage of their aircraft. This pleasant little lighthouse station was demanned and automated back in 1965.

Heading southwards, the next lighthouse we come to is that of Skervuile, also known as 'Iron Rock', situated in the Sound of Jura. Established in 1865, this lighthouse actually remained completely unlit for a full five years due to one of the periodic disputes which flared up between the Northern Lighthouse Board and the Board of Trade. Skervuile was also to become one of the earliest examples of a lighthouse being demanned and automated, achieving this status as early as 1945.

On the distillery-dotted island of Islay there are situated no less than three major lighthouses. The most northerly of these is Rhuba a Mhaill lighthouse which watches over the approaches to the narrow Sound of Islay between Islay and Jura, and flashes white/red every fifteen seconds. Rhuba a Mhaill, more commonly known by its angli-

Lismore lighthouse – '…the nearest parish church an inaccesible twelve miles away'.

Skervuile lighthouse, in the Sound of Jura

Ruvaal lighthouse.

cised name of Ruvaal, was constructed in 1859. As would happen a few years later at Skervuile, Ruvaal lighthouse was to be yet another subject of one of the many acrimonious disputes between the Northern Lighthouse Board and the Board of Trade over the issue of finances. In fact it is recorded that no less than 68 letters passed back and forth between the two authorities before the lighthouse was built, and when construction work finally started it was to be subject to swingeing economic cuts by the Board of Trade. The parsimony of the Board of Trade's financial policies was later to be derisively commented upon by the lightkeepers who complained that the dwelling houses at Ruvaal lighthouse were 'little better than dog kennels'. In a severe gale in 1883, the lightkeepers reported to Edinburgh that the cut price-built tower of the lighthouse oscillated in the strong wind. In its way still a victim of Board of Trade economic policy, Ruvaal was demanned and automated in 1986.

No More Paraffin-Oilers

Marking the southern end of the Sound of Jura, with a character of two white/red flashes every ten seconds, is the lighthouse of McArthur's Head established in 1861. I know little about this lighthouse (and have often wondered who McArthur was), except that the boatman and one of his crew were tragically drowned when their boat was swamped here in 1898. McArthur's Head lighthouse was demanned and automated in 1969.

On the small island of Orsay just off the south coast of the Rinns of Islay, is situated the Rinns of Islay lighthouse established in 1825. The 90-foot high white-painted tower, with its ornamental string courses, was constructed by the contractor John Gibb of Aberdeen at a cost of £8,000. The light displays a character of one white flash every five seconds. I have worked with several lightkeepers who have served at 'the Rinns', and I have heard nothing but good about this lighthouse and the shore station in Bowmore, Islay's principal town. Although the Rinns of Islay lightkeepers were withdrawn at an earlier date, this lighthouse was not considered fully automatic until early March 1998.

McArthur's Head lighthouse.

The Rinns of Islay lighthouse.

The scenic island of Arran is our next port of call. At the village of Lamlash looking out across the bay where, in 1263, King Hakon and his Norsemen moored their longships en route to an unpleasant shock at the battle of Largs, stands the lighthouse known as Holy Island Inner Light. This lighthouse was established in 1877, and originally just displayed a fixed green light. In 1894 the Holy Island Inner lightkeepers were responsible for the safe rescue of the crew of a ship called the *Ossian* which had been wrecked near to the lighthouse. In more recent times, this lighthouse was one of the first in Scotland to be fitted with an automatic fog detector. The station was demanned and automated in 1977.

Across Lamlash Bay on Holy Island itself is situated Holy Island Outer lighthouse, established in 1905 to supplement the Inner lighthouse. Holy Island Outer lighthouse has an architectural claim to fame, being the first square lighthouse tower to be constructed by the Northern Lighthouse Board. It was demanned and automated in 1977.

Around the corner from Lamlash Bay, and just off the southern tip of Arran is the low-lying island of Pladda. The lighthouse on Pladda was only the fifth to be constructed by the Northern Lighthouse Board, way back in 1790. The original lighthouse was extensively renovated and almost completely rebuilt between 1821 and 1830. Pladda was a rock lighthouse with the shore accommodation for the off-duty lightkeepers and their families being situated in Lamlash. The lighthouse, with its character of three white flashes every thirty seconds, was demanned and fully automated in 1989.

Pladda lighthouse.

'Campbeltown Loch I wish you were whisky' Andy Stewart used to sing. A sentiment which would no doubt have found agreement with the keepers who manned the lighthouse on the island of Davaar at the mouth of the loch. Although it was classed as a rock lighthouse, at low tide it was possible to walk from the mainland to Davaar across a shingle bar called the 'Dhorlin'. Displaying a character of two white flashes every ten seconds, Davaar lighthouse was established in 1854 and demanned and made fully automatic in 1989.

Not so many miles to the south of Davaar, lying just off the southeast tip of the Kintyre peninsula, is situated the small green island of Sanda with its lighthouse of the same name. West of Scotland shipowners campaigned for a lighthouse to be established on Sanda as early as 1825, when the *Christiana* of Glasgow was lost with all hands on the nearby Patterson's Rock, but it was to be twenty-five years before the lighthouse was finally constructed, in 1850. Sanda lighthouse station is a fairly unique piece of lighthouse architecture consisting of the 46 foot high lighthouse tower itself situated on the top of an eminence called the Ship Rock. Two smaller towers are stepped into the face of the rock with the stairway from the lightkeepers' dwelling houses nestling at the foot of the Ship Rock. In 1900 the Sanda boatman and his two sons were awarded the R.N.L.I. silver medal for saving the crew of a schooner which was wrecked near the lighthouse. Sanda, with its character of long flashing white/red every twenty-four seconds, was latterly an offshore rock lighthouse with the off-duty lightkeepers and their families living in accommodation in Campbeltown. The lighthouse was demanned and automated in March 1992.

On the south-west tip of the Kintyre peninsula is situated the second lighthouse to be constructed by the fledgling Northern Lighthouse Board way back in 1788, the lighthouse of the Mull of Kintyre. Although this lighthouse is situated on the Scottish

Davaar.

mainland, the actual engineering logistics of building in such a remote locality in 1788 were almost comparable to the later engineering feats of the constructions at Skerryvore and Dubh Artach. Delivering the building materials to the site by sea was rendered impossible because of the hazardous nature of the shoreline on which the lighthouse was being constructed. This meant that every single artifact used in the work had to be trekked across the barren moorland by pack horses from the base set up in Campbeltown, twelve miles distant. After a great deal of hard work, and what must have been countless journeys, the lighthouse was completed and the light exhibited for the first time in October 1788. Matthew Hardie, a local crofter, was the first of the many lightkeepers to serve at the Mull of Kintyre lighthouse. He was paid £50 per annum, with the usual grazing and fuel perks.

There was a slightly embarrassing shipwreck off the Mull of Kintyre lighthouse in 1895 when the Northern Lighthouse Board's own tender, the iron paddle steamer *Signal* ran aground on the rocks here in thick fog when en route to Sanda lighthouse. All crew and passengers were safely rescued but the *Signal* sank the following day. The squat tower of the Mull of Kintyre lighthouse is sited at the top of a 250-foot high cliff and at the foot of an impossibly steep gradient which hairpins down from the public road above. An old acquaintance of mine, Skye man Donald Macpherson, was an Assistant Lightkeeper here for some time. I recall him telling me the following anecdote regard-

Mull of Kintyre lighthouse.

ing this steep hill. He said 'One of the local men had a habit of calling at the house. He was a pleasant enough chap but once he got into the house you could not get rid of him, and despite the broadest hints he would sit yapping for hours. Well, one night the wife and I were settled in front of the telly when we heard a knock at the door. I said "Oh that will only be old so and so and I just can't be doing with him tonight. Just ignore it." Well, the knock came again and again, but we just ignored it. Then after a time it became quite frantic and I was finally forced to go to the door with the intention of seeing our man off in no uncertain terms. I yanked open the door, but to my surprise I could not see a soul there, and then I heard a low moaning noise coming from the ground at my feet. I looked down and I was horrified to see a complete stranger all covered in cuts and bruises lying in a heap on my doorstep. A battered and mangled wheelchair lay on its side near him where it had hit the side of the house with a hell of a clatter. Well the poor chap wasn't too badly hurt, and once I had got him inside and given him a cup of tea we both began to see the funny side of the situation. He hadn't realised just how steep the hill was down to the lighthouse and he had attempted to descend it in his wheelchair. How he had managed to negotiate the corners as the wheelchair began to run away, faster and faster would have been a sight worth beholding. He told me that he was quite relieved when he finally came to such a sudden stop against the wall of my house, as he had visions of flying clean off the top of the cliff and being catapulted into the Irish Sea, when he reached the bottom of the hill!'

That is one very steep hill indeed as I can personally verify having walked up and down it when I visited the Mull of Kintyre lighthouse on my marathon walk in 1986.

Mull of Kintyre lighthouse was made automatic on 31st March 1996. The existing 1st order lens rotated on a mercury bath pedestal was retained with the light source being a 400 watt metal halide lamp. This set-up is powered by batteries trickle-charged from the mains electric and monitored via PSTN to Edinburgh.

Leaving Kintyre, we head south-easterly into the middle of the Firth of Clyde where we come across the distinctive profile of Paddy's Milestone, the granite mass of Ailsa Craig. The lighthouse was established on Ailsa Craig in 1886 and was something of an innovation as the place was purposely constructed as a gas-powered light. The gas was manufactured on the island by the lightkeepers by the process of heating mineral oil with coal in retorts. The gas produced by this process was stored on the island in two gasometers. Due to his qualifications as a trained plumber, and the vast amount of piping involved with Ailsa Craig's gas-powered lighthouse, lightkeeper Alexander Thompson was stationed for 35 years at this one lighthouse, finally retiring from here in 1921. Thompson even got married on the island to the daughter of his first Principal Lightkeeper. I found it interesting to read that as long ago as 1886, when Ailsa Craig lighthouse was established, one of the first problems encountered by the lightkeepers was that of excursionists travelling out from Girvan and making a nuisance of themselves at the lighthouse.

Opinions about the desirability of visitors to the lighthouse vary quite widely among lightkeepers at the various lighthouses. We saw so few visitors on Stroma that we did

Paddy's milestone – Ailsa Craig.

not seriously mind them and usually, if asked nicely, someone would find the time to take them up the tower and show them around the station. However, there is the other side of the coin. I recall visiting Cape Wrath lighthouse during the course of my walk. I found that a bus load of visitors to the Cape were arriving at the lighthouse from the ferry almost every half hour or so. The lightkeepers had every building at the station securely locked up and they were sitting in the living room in the accommodation block, putting me in mind of a bunch of Wild West settlers being besieged by the Indians.

When I was at Neist Point lighthouse, Principal lightkeeper Donald Macleod had a 'Wet Paint' sign which he would affix to the tower door every morning in summer. 'Them buggers will pinch anything that is not tied down!' was Donald's attitude to visitors. However, some lightkeepers have been known to take a more enterprising view of things. There was one particular lighthouse, situated near a popular holiday resort, where the keepers exploited the tourist situation to the full having their particular routine off to a fine art. The Principal lightkeeper would dress up in his best civilian suit after his dinner and head for one of the public bars in the town which was popular with the trippers. Once in the pub he would strike up a conversation with the holidaymakers in the course of which he would casually mention that he had heard that a visit to the local lighthouse nearby was well worth a trip. Organising a sizeable party he would lead them like the Pied Piper of Hamelin up to the lighthouse where he would call out the lightkeeper on duty. Not letting on that he knew the man, he would politely ask him if they might be shown around the lighthouse, to which the duty lightkeeper would readily agree. After the tour was over the incognito Principal would loudly proclaim that the visit had been the high spot of his holiday, and pulling out his wallet, would give the duty lightkeeper a fiver for his trouble. Of course, the trippers would generously follow his lead and the duty lightkeeper would eventually end up with quite a tidy sum for his hour or so's work. Later that day the spoils would be divvied up along with the return of the original fiver!

At another lighthouse they were at least a little bit more subtle. Here the lightkeepers would merely leave a lighthouse uniform cap prominently displayed on a table at the entrance to the tower, in which a fifty pence piece had been placed for encouragement. This practice came to an abrupt end one day when someone pinched the cap, and the fifty pence. As Donald Macleod would say: 'Them buggers …' etc!

But to return to Ailsa Craig lighthouse. In the days before radio communications were installed at offshore lighthouses, an experiment was undertaken here using carrier pigeons to take messages ashore to Girvan. Unfortunately this turned out to be a failure as the poor pigeons were steadily picked off by the predatory hawks which nested on the rock. A latter day problem at Ailsa Craig was rats. The rock became quite infested with them and periodically the lightkeepers would organise a bit of entertainment by holding a Grand Rat Hunt. I worked for a time with an ex-Ailsa Craig Principal lightkeeper, Shetlander Ron Birnie. There is a popular notion among the general public that the majority of lightkeepers spend most of their spare time at the lighthouse industriously inserting model sailing ships into empty bottles. Ron is the only lightkeeper I met who indulged in this particular hobby, and a beautiful job he made of it too. But Ron thought big and he progressed from miniature *Cutty Sarks* in empty whisky bottles to constructing intricate and superbly detailed models of North Sea oil rigs. He enclosed these models in the glass bulbs of the outsized electric lamps used to illuminate the lighthouse light.

Rapidly winking its six white flashes every thirty seconds, Ailsa Craig lighthouse is now completely automatic having been demanned in 1990.

Returning to the mainland, the next lighthouse we visit is that of Turnberry Point on the Ayrshire coast. This lighthouse was constructed in 1873 on the site of an ancient castle which reputedly once belonged to Robert the Bruce's mother. This lighthouse is situated in a prime position, being slap-bang in the middle of the famous Turnberry golf course. The nearby hole, (I forget which number), is even called 'The Lighthouse'. Due to its locality, Turnberry Point has long been a popular posting with those lightkeepers keen on the 'Royal and Ancient Game'. A further bonus was that the Turnberry lightkeepers were kindly granted honorary membership of the golf club during the time that they worked at the lighthouse, and consequently they were granted free access to the excellent links. I paid a call to Turnberry Point lighthouse during my marathon walk in 1986. When I arrived it was just a week or so before the start of the Open, being held at Turnberry that year, and the place was bustling with preparations for this grand event. Assistant lightkeeper Norman Douglas and his wife hospitably put me up for the night at the lighthouse. A few weeks later I was to hear some news

Turnberry Point lighthouse – ideal for golfing lightkeepers.

about Norman. A couple of days after my visit he was approached by a wealthy American who offered him and his wife a not inconsiderable sum of money plus free accommodation in a top Glasgow hotel, on the condition that Norman agreed to let him have the use of his house for the duration of the Open. Of course the Northern Lighthouse Board would have taken a pretty dim view of the matter had Norman agreed and they later found out. But they need not have worried; Norman was probably an even greater golf fanatic than that American! Turnberry Point lighthouse was demanned and automated in 1987 and numerous golfing lightkeepers heaved a sorry sigh. It is interesting to think that this prime site will be worth much more than any of the lightkeepers who have lived here and carefully tended the buildings for 114 years might be able to afford.

At the narrow neck of the Rinns of Galloway is sited the 46 foot high white tower of Loch Ryan lighthouse, established here in 1847. This lighthouse became a one man-operated light way back in 1897, and would seem to have been something of a quiet backwater. Loch Ryan lighthouse was eventually completely demanned and automated in 1964.

On the rocky northern tip of the Rinns of Galloway stands the tall tower of the lighthouse at Corsewall Point, established in 1816 in response to the increase in shipping trade from the ports of Greenock, Glasgow and Liverpool. I called in at Corsewall Point during the course of my marathon walk in 1986 and was regally entertained by Principal Lightkeeper Hector Lamont and his wife. I recall that I noticed that one of the lightkeepers at that time had an enterprising hobby – he was building his own autogyro. I have often wondered if this contraption ever got off the ground, and thought what grand uses such a machine might be put to at an offshore lighthouse. Corsewall Point, with its character of alternate long flashing white and red every 74 seconds, was automated on 31st March 1994. However, the character of the light was altered to five white flashes every thirty seconds. The automatic system is powered by batteries trickle-charged from the mains. In the event of a power failure the batteries can maintain the light for 36 hours. If this is insufficient time for the mains power to be restored, a less powerful emergency light with an endurance of two weeks will come into action. The lightkeepers houses were sold off and the station has been turned into a hotel.

On the northern tip of the picturesque little haven of Portpatrick can be found the lighthouse of Killantringan, established here by the Northern Lighthouse Board in 1900. Killantringan lighthouse is a quiet and peaceful place, appearing as a splash of white against a green backdrop of rolling farmland. This peace and tranquillity was, however, rudely interrupted on the morning of February 26th 1982 when the container ship the *Craigantlet* ran aground in a storm onto the rocks at the foot of the lighthouse. The ship was laden with a cargo of dangerous chemicals and after the stranding some of this devil's brew began to leak out from the damaged containers in which it was stored. Scientists were called in and they quickly declared that the wreck was a serious health hazard and ordered the evacuation of the Killantringan lighthouse. The lightkeepers and their families were moved out and accommodated in a Stranraer

Corsewall lighthouse – taken from a Harrier Jump Jet.

hotel. It was to be a full six weeks before it was considered safe enough for them to re-occupy their lighthouse homes. Two years later Killantringan lighthouse witnessed another evacuation, but this time for good, as the lighthouse had been demanned and made fully automatic. The distinguishing character of Killantringan is two white flashes every fifteen seconds.

In the most southerly corner of Scotland at the tip of the Rinns of Galloway is situated the towering headland of the Mull of Galloway. It was from the summit of this high headland that legend says the last two Gallovidian Picts jumped to their deaths rather than reveal the secret recipe of heather ale to the invading Scots. The light-house here was constructed in 1830 at a cost of £9,000. This was yet another port of call during my walk in 1986. The Principal Lightkeeper then at the Mull of Galloway lighthouse was John Lamont, one of three brothers in the lighthouse service and all with the rank of Principal. Brother Hector had entertained me at Corsewall, and the

81

Mull of Galloway lighthouse.

third brother Murdoch was then Principal Lightkeeper at Neist Point on Skye. With its character of one white flash every twenty seconds, the Mull of Galloway lighthouse was demanned and automated in 1988.

The final lighthouse situated on the south-western seaboard of Scotland is the lighthouse of Little Ross sited at the mouth of Kirkcudbright Bay. Little Ross lighthouse was established by the Northern Lighthouse Board in 1843 after a petition signed by nearly 400 people 'interested in the navigation of the Solway Firth' was presented to the House of Commons. This lighthouse gained a certain notoriety in Scottish lighthouse history when in 1960, Assistant Lightkeeper Robert Dickson robbed and killed the 64 year old Occasional Lightkeeper Hugh Clarke. Dickson was eventually apprehended by the police for what the press labelled at the time 'the perfect murder'. At his trial he was sentenced to be hanged but this was commuted to life imprisonment. He later took his own life in prison. As if in shame for the dark deed committed here, later that same year Little Ross lighthouse was demanned and automated. It was the first lighthouse to enter into the huge automation programme which is now complete.

6

The North East

The first lighthouse we visit on Scotland's north-eastern coastline was yet another subject of a nineteenth century dispute between the Commissioners of the Northern Lighthouse Board, the Board of Trade and the Elder Brethren of Trinity House. A lighthouse was proposed for siting on the Caithness coast near to the busy herring fishing port of Wick. After conducting a survey of the area, the Northern Lighthouse Board decided that Sarclet Head to the south of Wick was the best place to site such a light. However, the Elder Brethren stepped in and insisted that Noss Head north of Wick, overlooking Sinclair's Bay, was where they had decided that the new lighthouse should be situated. The Commissioners felt so strongly about the matter that they went to the lengths of petitioning Queen Victoria in council with their case. This action brought the Board of Trade into the argument, who, as they invariably did, backed the Elder Brethren. The lighthouse was to be sited at Noss Head. Work commenced on Noss Head lighthouse and the light was exhibited for the first time in 1849. In 1987 it was demanned and fully automated. The last Principal Lightkeeper at Noss Head was Sandy Strachan, a kind-hearted man who, I remember, urged me to take a packet of sweets from him 'for the road' when I called in there during my walk in 1986. His Assistant Lightkeeper, Ian Longmuir, was transferred to join our crew when I was on Stroma.

It is not hard to imagine the frustration the Commissioners of the Northern Lighthouse Board must have often felt throughout much of the nineteenth century over the interference of Trinity House in their affairs. This older lighthouse service was often prone to act as 'elder brethren' and treat the younger organisation very much as the new boy who did not know what was best for him. National conflict must have come into the disputes as well. The Northern Lighthouse Board had specifically been titled 'Northern' and not 'Scottish', in the spirit of the Act of Union of 1707 which regarded Scotland as North Britain. But then you must remember that the Commissioners were almost all legal men, and it was this profession in Scotland which had always been well to the fore in the protection of Scottish identity and traditions and rights. This is still in evidence today in that we retain our own legal system in Scotland which is substantially different to that in operation south of the border. How they must have muttered to themselves in angry frustration about 'English interference', and when the London-based Board of Trade invariably took the part of Trinity House, 'English collusion'!

At least in the siting of the next lighthouse we visit, we find that the Commissioners were fully vindicated in their original choice of Sarclet Head rather than Noss Head. With the outbreak of the First World War, and the subsequent increase in Royal Navy shipping passing to and fro from the naval anchorage at Scapa Flow, it quickly became evident that a second light was required for this part of the Caithness coastline. In answer to this demand, the lighthouse of Clyth Ness just south of Wick was established in 1916. It was a lighthouse construction which would have been unnecessary had the Commissioners got their own way back in 1849, and built at Sarclet Head. The distinctive red-banded tower of Clyth Ness lighthouse was demanned and became fully automatic in 1964.

In what was described at the time as 'the Moray Firth hurricane', a fearsome storm in 1826, sixteen vessels were lost and this led to the construction of Tarbat Ness lighthouse. This 130 foot tower with its twin red bands, was constructed in 1830 by the contractor John Smith of Inverness. It might be argued that this was the site, albeit briefly, of Scotland's first one-man light. It was roughly on the present site of the lighthouse where the Brahn Seer was burnt alive in a tar barrel by the Duchess of Seaforth! The records of Tarbat Ness lighthouse report that the lighthouse was subjected to an earth tremor late last century. The records show that the tremor was strong enough to rattle the shades and the lamp glasses. Jack Clark was the last Principal Lightkeeper at Tarbat Ness lighthouse when it was demanned and automated in 1985. The light has a character of four white flashes every thirty seconds.

At the entrance to the Firth of Inverness is sited the lighthouse of Chanonry Point established in 1846. I read with interest that during a visit here by the Commissioners in 1886, it was found that the clocks at the lighthouse station differed by a whole thirty minutes from Greenwich Mean Time. In those days, before accurate time signals and the 'speaking clock' was invented, setting the lighthouse clock to the proper time was a complicated business involving a sundial. Sundials are still to be found to this day at the majority of lighthouses.

Quoting from the original lighthouse General Order of 1852, the procedure was stated to be as follows:

Clyth Ness lighthouse on the Caithness coast
(Photograph courtesy of Liam Whittles).

Chanonry Point lighthouse.

'The Principal keeper shall go to the dial, when the sun is shining, and shall watch until the shadow of the style touches any hour, half-hour or other time agreed beforehand with the Assistant, who shall stand on the balcony, waiting for a signal from the Principal. The Principal shall then make the signal, on seeing which, the Assistant shall immediately set the timepiece to the time already agreed upon. The Principal shall then take a note from the Table of Equation of Time engraved on the sundial, of the number of minutes by which the clock should differ from the time given by the dial; and shall afterwards proceed at once to the lightroom where he shall put the timepiece back or forward according as the clock shall be slower or faster than the sun at the time'.

As late as 1920 the problem of accurate timing had still not been satisfactorily solved as can be seen from an incident which occurred on Stroma. In the early morning of 2nd July 1920 the 1,613 ton steamer *Grayson* of New York ran aground on Stroma in thick fog. According to the islanders the *Grayson* ran aground at 3.52 a.m., but the lighthouse records show that the foghorn at the lighthouse was not started until 4.05 a.m. At the subsequent inquiry the lightkeepers were cleared of the charge of not sounding the horn during the fog when it was discovered that the time given by the islanders was 'Local Apparent Time' with a discrepancy of some twenty-five minutes between it and the Greenwich Mean Time being used at the lighthouse.

Chanonry Point was downgraded to a one-man-operated light in 1900 and I have often wondered how he managed to set the lightroom clock by the sundial on his own. The lighthouse was finally demanned and automated in 1985.

In 1846, the lighthouse at Cromarty on the northern tip of the Black Isle was established. Primely situated on the edge of the town of Cromarty itself, this lighthouse was always a popular posting, but like its neighbour at Chanonry Point it too was demanned and automated in 1985. The character of the light at Chanonry Point is occulting white every six seconds while that at Cromarty is occulting (i.e cut off at regular intervals), red/white every ten seconds.

Situated amidst banks of yellow-flowering gorse bushes, and overlooking the fishing port of Lossiemouth, is found the lighthouse of Covesea Skerries, established in 1846. The headland where this lighthouse is sited was called 'Halliman Head' reflecting the local legend that the Holy man St. Geradine used to display a lantern at this point to warn shipping. St. Geradine is commemorated on the coat of arms of the town of Lossiemouth in which he is depicted brandishing his warning lantern at a passing ship. Covesea Skerries lighthouse was demanned and automated in 1984, but the Northern Lighthouse Board decided not to sell off the dwelling houses but to retain them and use the station as a holiday home for their staff. As a lightkeeper spending half my life living and working at a lighthouse, I confess that I thought that this would be the last place I would choose to spend my holidays! However, when I visited Covesea Skerries during the course of my marathon walk, I was pleasantly surprised by the facilities there.

Cromarty lighthouse.

Covesea lighthouse on Halliman Head.

Kinnaird Head lighthouse overlooking Fraserburgh's bustling harbour has an important place in the history of Scottish lighthouses. When the light here was first exhibited on 1st December 1787, Kinnaird Head lighthouse became the Northern Lighthouse Board's very first operational station. Employed to man the first lighthouse was the first lightkeeper, a north-east shipmaster by the name of James Park who was paid a shilling a night for his trouble on the condition that he had another person with him every night whom he was to instruct in the matter of cleaning the lantern and lighting the lamps. Kinnaird Head lighthouse is built on top of the aptly, if not very imaginatively, named Tower Castle, which was purchased by the Commissioners from Lord Saltoun for the then inflated price of £1,800 (which would have kept James Park tending the light for 36,000 nights!). This 16th century castle is still an integral part of the lighthouse, and at one time contained the accommodation for visiting lightkeepers and the Local or Occasional lightkeeper when either of them was on watch at the lighthouse. I stayed here in 1986, and it was a slightly odd sensation to sleep in the roomy top floor of an old castle with the lighthouse lightroom just up the stairs above my head. Back in 1787, mariners reported that the light from the new Kinnaird Head lighthouse was visible in clear weather up to a range of 14 miles. In March 1929 the range of Kinnaird Head lighthouse was vastly increased by other means when it became the first Northern Lighthouse Board installation to be fitted with a permanent radio beacon. After a total of 204 years as a continuously manned lighthouse, Kinnaird

Head, with its character of one white flash every fifteen seconds, was finally demanned and automated in 1991. It now forms the home for Scotland's Lighthouse Museum.

Just to the north of Peterhead, off the sand-dune dotted Buchan coast, is situated the offshore lighthouse of Rattray Head. Constructed from granite quarried at Rubislaw, the twin levels of the 120-foot high lighthouse were constructed on the tidal Ron Rock in 1895. A peculiarity of Rattray Head lighthouse was that the station's boatman was, in fact, a tractor driver! With this lighthouse situated barely half a mile off shore, the place could easily be reached at low tide across the glistening sand flats, and the relief was carried out here by tractor and trailer. When I was a Supernumerary lightkeeper, I spent my first Christmas and New Year at Rattray lighthouse. A more dreary dismal place to spend the festive season would be hard to find. Although the company was fine, I found Rattray Head lighthouse itself a dingy, damp, cramped place in which to live and work. The engine room, which was situated in the larger lower levels of the lighthouse, had walls running and discoloured with damp on which glistened salt crystals. The general odour in most of the lower levels of the lighthouse was that of the exposed sea bottom when the tide is well ebbed. I recall cleaning the lens in the lightroom one forenoon during my stay at Rattray Head lighthouse. While polishing away I noticed a perfectly round hole in the corner of the thick glass of one of the prisms, which I pointed out to Principal lightkeeper Len Fraser. Len nonchalantly replied: 'Oh aye. That's a machine gun bullet hole.' Apparently in the dark days of 1940, a coastal convoy was wrecked near the lighthouse and a number of enemy aircraft launched an attack on the helpless stranded ships. One of these aircraft decided to divert its attention to the lighthouse. Dropping three bombs which narrowly missed, the aircraft followed up by strafing the lantern with machine gun fire. A short time later the damage to the lantern and lightroom was repaired with the replacement of panes of glass in the lantern and shattered prisms in the lens were taken out and renewed. Apparently the prism which I had been industriously polishing had failed to shatter when struck by a single machine gun bullet which left a hole in its corner. As this did not affect the efficiency of the prism it was left in place and provided a grim reminder of World War Two.

The Christmas dinner at Rattray Head lighthouse that year was a tasty affair, in which no small credit was afforded to the excellent brandy butter concocted by Principal Len Fraser following a quick raid on the first aid box! In fact, I discovered during my years in the lighthouse service that the standard of cuisine at the lighthouses was normally pretty good. Not slanted so much towards gourmet or cordon bleu, but good, plain, honest grub. The usual routine at an offshore lighthouse was that the two Assistant lightkeepers took turn about in assuming the duties of cook, usually a week at a time. The Principal lightkeeper had the perk of being excused this particular job although I have known some who have liked to keep their hand in, particularly if there was a dirty job to do elsewhere in the lighthouse that week. The cook would be responsible for preparing and serving the main meal of the day which was usually eaten at about one o'clock. His other domestic duties included keeping the kitchen and living quarters clean and tidy. As regards the other meals, breakfast was made by the man who was up on the early morning watch, and although at some lighthouses the crew all sat down to tea at five o'clock, cooked by the man on the afternoon watch, at the Muckle Flugga when I was there and presently on Stroma, tea operated on a help yourself basis. I presume to speak for the majority of lightkeepers in saying that they were, like myself, inexperienced in cooking when they joined the service and found themselves thrown in at the culinary deep end. I love the story which is told about the conversation between the old Principal lightkeeper and the brand new Supernumerary, which supposedly goes something like this:

Principal: 'Can you cook, boy?'

Supernumerary: 'No.'

Principal: 'Can you boil water?'

Supernumerary: 'Yes.'

Principal: 'You can cook!'

It was pretty much the same with me, and I learned chiefly from my mistakes. I remember serving up one of my first dinners at Neist Point lighthouse, a pretty watery and anaemic-looking mince and tatties.

'Did you remember to brown the mince, Ian?' asked Principal Donald Macleod, gingerly prodding the soggy mass on his plate with a fork. 'Er, it was pretty brown to start with,' I mumbled. But as time went on cooking lost its mystery and I gradually improved. In fact, nowadays I do most of the cooking when I am at home as well. Mind you, there are some who have bigger problems than others. I recall a Supernumerary who came to work with us on the Muckle Flugga, who we quickly realised might give us problems. He volunteered to go and make the coffee once we had got everything stowed away after the relief. After a couple of minutes he came out of the kitchen loudly complaining that somebody had removed the label with the instructions on it off the side of the instant coffee jar!

But back to Rattray Head lighthouse. Another peculiarity which struck me about this place was the situation of the lighthouse shore station. Most of the offshore lighthouses at which I had worked had their shore stations situated at least several miles from the actual lighthouse. For example, the Hyskeir and Skerryvore lighthouses had their shore stations situated in Oban; the Forth lightkeepers had their homes ashore in Granton, Edinburgh. But here at Rattray Head you could actually see the shore station on the sea front, about a mile from the lighthouse. Alas, this is all part of history now as Rattray Head lighthouse with its character of three white flashes every thirty seconds, was demanned and became fully automatic in 1982.

On the rocky foreshore of the village of Boddan just south of Peterhead, can be found the red-striped lighthouse which marks Scotland's most easterly point, that of Buchan Ness. John Gibb, contractor of Aberdeen, built the lighthouse here for the Northern Lighthouse Board in 1827, and this was the very first lighthouse in Scotland to be fitted with a flashing light. During World War Two, the Buchan Ness keepers discovered that there were hazards other than air raids when, on two separate occasions, drifting mines were blown on shore onto the rocks by the lighthouse, and exploded. Fortunately they caused no damage or injuries but gave all concerned a nasty fright. When I was a Supernumerary Lightkeeper, Buchan Ness lighthouse was the downfall of two of my contemporaries who both found the proximity of Boddam's public houses too much of a temptation. In latter years the lighthouse was a popular visiting venue for members of the staff of nearby R.A.F. Buchan. John Malcolm was the last Principal Lightkeeper here when the light was demanned and automated on his retirement from the service in 1987. Buchan Ness lighthouse displays a character of one white flash every five seconds.

Towering above the golf course on the Aberdeen shoreline can be found the tall, slim, elegant tower of Girdle Ness lighthouse. This was another lighthouse which was constructed by the Aberdeen contractor John Gibb back in 1833. This lighthouse was finally established after twenty years of agitation for one to be sited here, by the shipmasters of Aberdeen. They began their vociferous campaign in 1813 when the whaling ship *Oscar* was lost off Girdle Ness with only two men, out of a crew of forty-five, managing to struggle to shore. For many years the provision of a bit of ground to use as a garden plot for growing vegetables was regarded as a necessary perk by the lightkeepers, and encouraged by the Commissioners who advocated self-sufficiency.

An old engraving of Girdle Ness lighthouse.

In 1880, the Girdle Ness lightkeepers became so incensed with the poor quality of the garden ground at the lighthouse, that they sent a profit and loss account to the Lighthouse Board. There are no gardens, poor or otherwise at Girdle Ness now. With its character of two white flashes every twenty seconds, Girdle Ness lighthouse was demanned and made fully automatic in 1991.

South of Stonehaven, and a couple of miles along the coast from the picturesque little village of Catterline, you will find the lighthouse of Tod Head which was established in 1897. I visited this lighthouse during my walk in 1986 and it is not an easy place to get to. I got lost more than once among the winding, single track roads which lead up to the place. Though, in retrospect, my poor sense of direction at the time might have been partially to blame for my spending an hour in the excellent 'Creel Inn' in Catterline! Set amidst rich farmland, Tod Head lighthouse struck me at the time as being a nice quiet little backwater compared to the majority of the lighthouses in this area which seem to be situated either in or near busy fishing harbours. The late Magnus Pearson was the Principal Lightkeeper here at the time, and he justifiably took great pride in showing me around his immaculately kept lighthouse station. Tod Head was demanned and automated two years later in 1988. The light here displays a character of four white flashes every thirty seconds.

Tod Head lighthouse.

Near the village of Ferryden, about a mile along the road from the South Esk Hotel, once the famous 'Diamond Lil's' and probably the last establishment in Scotland to recognise decimal currency, is situated the lighthouse of Scurdie Ness. The 120 foot high tower with its light which displays a character of three white flashes every thirty seconds, was established in 1870 for the purpose of guiding shipping to the entrance of the Montrose basin. During World War Two, after a couple of heavy air raids on Montrose, there was an altercation at Scurdie Ness between the locals and the lightkeepers. The locals accused the lightkeepers of using their lighthouse to signal to the enemy and to guide the bombers onto their target. The R.A.F. became involved, and while absolving the poor lightkeepers of any hint of treason, had to point out that the brightly painted white tower did present the German bombers with an excellent landmark, and that it should be painted black. A couple of days later a Royal Navy detachment arrived at the lighthouse with orders to paint the tower black, but when they saw the ramshackle bosun's chair which the keepers used each year when they lime-washed the tower, there was a minor mutiny and the matelots point-blank refused to do the job, and so it was left to the lightkeepers themselves! In fact, several lighthouses were thus treated during the war. The black paint was made up by mixing soot and coal dust with the limewash which was normally used. I visited Scurdie Ness during my lighthouse walk in 1986, and was very hospitably entertained there by Principal Lightkeeper Bob Duthie and his wife. Bob was the last lightkeeper at this lighthouse as Scurdie Ness was demanned and made fully automatic in the following year of 1987.

Scurdie Ness.

7

The Firth of Forth and South East Scotland

Situated eleven miles from the coast and in the centre of the busy shipping ap proaches to the Firth of Tay and the Firth of Forth, the Inchcape Reef was a cer tain contender for a lighthouse. The Bell Rock, covered by up to sixteen feet of sea water at high tide, had claimed countless ships over the years. With an added sense of urgency brought about by the loss, with all hands, of the 64-gun warship *HMS York* in January 1804, the Commissioners of the Northern Lighthouse Board resolved to do something about the matter.

The Board's engineer, Robert Stevenson, was chosen to be the man responsible for the construction of the Bell Rock lighthouse. The only other example of a similar construction, on such an exposed site off the British mainland, was Smeaton's building of the Eddystone lighthouse. The Eddystone lighthouse was built on rocks just covered by the tide at high water, while the proposed Bell Rock lighthouse would have to be built on rocks which were barely dry at low water! Stevenson soon realised that he would have a job and a half on his hands. With Smeaton's 'Narrative' as a rough guide, the thirty-five year old Robert Stevenson designed a tower which, when completed, would be 100 feet in height and constructed from granite quarried at Rubislaw, which was pre-cut and shaped by masons ashore before being shipped out to the Bell Rock.

Work commenced on the foundations in August 1807 with the men working as long as possible on the site at low water before being forced off by the rising tide. They would then be rowed away to wait on board the floating lightship *Pharos*. This was an ex-Prussian fishing boat, the *Tonge Gerrit*, which had been captured as a prize of war in the Napoleonic conflict which was raging at that time. In fact, the needs of the Royal Navy in the Napoleonic wars were to have such an effect on the construction work that seamen involved in the building of the Bell Rock lighthouse were issued with special medals of exemption to save them from the predations of the press gangs which nightly scoured the dockyards of Leith. In July 1808 the foundation stone was laid with much ceremony. This was quickly followed by the laying of the first course of the lighthouse which consisted of 123 stones weighing 104 tons in total. The entire foundations of the lighthouse consisted of 400 stones with a total weight of over 385 tons. All of these were shipped out to the site by lighter.

Stevenson had constructed a temporary beacon on the rock, and in 1809 he built a wooden barrack upon this which enabled his workmen to labour almost continuously on the steadily rising tower. Access between the barrack and the tower was by means of a Jacob's ladder. The men christened the barrack 'Hurricane House'. The construction of this barrack was no doubt partially instigated by a near-disastrous incident which befell Stevenson and thirty workmen who found themselves at the mercy of the rising tide with one of their boats cast adrift. The remaining boats had insufficient room on board for everyone to be taken off safely. That rescue did arrive at the eleventh hour, was purely by chance. This little drama in the history of the construction of the Bell Rock lighthouse, is commemorated in the name of one of the rocks which make up the Inchcape. It bears the poignant title of 'The Last Hope'. In 1810, the remaining courses of pre-cut stones were laid to complete the tower, and the final fitting out work was done. On the night of 1st February 1811, in the charge of Principal Lightkeeper John Reid, the light was exhibited for the first time.

Robert Stevenson and his men had, to my mind, accomplished one of the finest engineering feats ever attempted in Scotland with the building of this lighthouse. The tower complete with lantern, stands 115 feet high and is 42 feet in diameter at the base, tapering to 15 feet at the top below the lighthouse balcony. The first 30 feet of the tower consist of solid dovetailed masonry, and above that are five compartments and the lantern chamber. The volume of masonry in the tower amounts to 28,530 cubic feet with a total weight of 2,076 tons. The total expense of the enterprise, plus the cost of the dwelling houses for the lightkeepers in Ladyloan, Arbroath, came to the then huge sum of £61,331 9s 2d and this was in the days when whisky sold for eleven shillings a gallon! Considering the difficult and hazardous nature of the construction of the Bell Rock lighthouse, accidents and casualties were remarkably few and there was only one fatality. This was a young boy who fell to his death off the Jacob's ladder. I once had the opportunity of reading Stevenson's diary of the days of construction and commenting later on this incident, he says that although it was the boy's own fault for skylarking, he took pity on his mother who had recently also lost her husband at the battle of Waterloo. As the dead boy would have been the family's chief bread-winner, he was prepared to take on the next eldest son as a replacement. Unfortunately, the mother's thoughts on this are not recorded!

Two years after the Bell Rock lighthouse was completed, a signal tower was constructed on the sea front at Arbroath for the purpose of communication by means of visual signals. This signal tower was converted into the Bell Rock lighthouse museum. I believe that on display there was a life-size dummy of one of the Bell Rock's last Principal lightkeepers which gives visitors a taped commentary. After the Bell Rock was demanned and automated, the Principal lightkeeper on whom the dummy was modelled was transferred to Stroma lighthouse, on the opposite four week watch to myself. One of our Assistant lightkeepers did not have a very high opinion of this gentleman, and he commented to me one day that he was quite convinced that the dummy was sometimes sent out to Stroma while the man himself remained on shore!

The Bell Rock (photograph courtesy of Christopher Nicholson).

I worked two spells of duty on the Bell Rock lighthouse when I was a Supernumerary lightkeeper. Actually just getting to the lighthouse itself was quite an unforgettable experience. I sailed out for the first time on board the lighthouse tender *Pharos* which I had boarded the previous evening in Leith. The *Pharos* used to be the flagship of the Northern Lighthouse Board's fleet of three tenders, but she was sold off a couple of years ago. Now renamed the *Amazing Grace,* and in new livery, she ferries rich tourists around the Caribbean. Lucky old *Pharos*! It's a far cry from the bleak, cold winter's day when I sailed out on her to the Bell Rock. Once we had arrived in the vicinity of the lighthouse, a ship's boat was launched to take the provisions and myself to the narrow metal grill landing which served the Bell Rock. The short boat trip was quite an eye-opener as the seaman in charge deftly steered the wooden launch along a twisting and deviating course through, and occasionally just skimming the kelp-festooned rocks and ledges which make up the Inchcape Reef. Once we had secured at the landing, everything moved at speed as the Bell Rock keepers hurried to get the provisions and stores safely into the tower in a race against the incoming tide. I will never forget the peculiar sensation I experienced when all had been safely gathered into the tower and I stood alone on the metal grill of the landing with the icy waves lapping around my ankles. Looking around I could see nothing but the grey, empty sea all around me. It made me feel very small and insignificant in the great scheme of things.

That relief day had thankfully been a fine calm one but during my first week I was to experience the entirely different sensation of living in a pillar-rock lighthouse at the height of a severe North Sea storm. The most unforgettable and frightening sensation is the deep resonant boom and shudder you feel when the wind-whipped rollers break against the slim tower of the lighthouse. The television flickers and the crockery in the kitchen-cum-living room rattles faintly as the whole tower vibrates. It can be a bit unsettling until you get used to it, and some people never do. Visibility out of the small windows set in the tower is virtually nil as the air outside is filled with whirling spray and foam, giving the appearance of a raging white-out blizzard. This lack of view adds to the feeling of claustrophobia in the cramped confines of the tower where you find yourself living in a strange vertical dimension.

In such a cramped and confined environment as the Bell Rock lighthouse, it is a major asset if you have the company of a good crew of lightkeepers who all get on well together. I must admit that both times I was at the Bell Rock I found the lightkeepers there excellent company and generally full of good humour. I could give numerous examples of the kind of mischief that they got up to, but one in particular comes to mind. This is what happened to the Local lightkeeper a couple of months before my first visit to the place. The toilet at the Bell Rock lighthouse consists of little more than a bucket-like contraption situated in a compartment scarcely larger than a cupboard at the base of the tower. Due to the inconvenience of getting to this 'convenience', particularly during the night, the keepers were in the habit of keeping a suitable tin can with the lid cut off, near at hand in their bedrooms in case they should be caught short during the night. One night, the peace and tranquillity of the lighthouse was shattered by a scream of anguish emanating from the Local lightkeeper's bedroom. He had gone to bed earlier, but unable to sleep because of a certain nagging discomfort, he had risen in the dark, fumbled for his tin can, located it and been happily engrossed in filling it when he suddenly felt his bare feet becoming warm and wet! Some joker had carefully removed the bottom out of the can earlier that day!

It was midsummer the next time I was at the Bell Rock lighthouse, and once again I found myself subjected to booms and shudders but this time it was not the weather to blame but high explosives. Salvage divers were working on the wreck of the First World War cruiser *HMS Argyll* which had run aground on the Inchcape Reef in October 1915. Parts of the wrecked cruiser were visible from the lighthouse at low water, including the remains of one of the huge gun turrets. Due to wartime conditions, the Bell Rock light was only lit on request during the First World War. On the night of 27th October 1915, a signal was sent to the Navy requesting that the Bell Rock light might be exhibited as the cruiser *Argyll* was due to be passing through the area on her way to Rosyth. But the signal was never received by the lighthouse and at four o'clock in the morning of the 28th, the horrified lightkeepers in their unlit lighthouse heard the terrible grinding crash as the cruiser hit the reef. Despite the bad weather, the quick arrival of the support ships and, what was later termed the 'extraordinary bravery' of the Bell Rock lightkeepers, ensured that not one member of the total ship's complement of 658 was lost during the rescue operation.

On a summer's day it was pleasant to sit in the lantern room of the Bell Rock lighthouse on an off-duty afternoon. The glass panes of the lantern turned the place into a huge solarium and through them you could idly watch the passing shipping while you basked in the sun. I was sitting thus, enjoying the sunshine one afternoon, when I happened to notice above my head an ugly dent in the otherwise smooth surface of the black-painted copper dome. I pointed it out to Principal Lightkeeper Jimmy Burns and he told me this tragic story. Back in 1955 helicopters from R.A.F. Leuchars on the mainland would quite often fly out to the lighthouse on training flights. Hovering alongside the tower, the R.A.F. crews would frequently lower newspapers and occasional fresh provisions to the keepers standing on the balcony. Disaster struck one day when a helicopter drifted too close and the rotor blades stuck in the tower dome, thus creating the ugly dented scar I had noticed. The stricken aircraft had plummeted like a stone onto the wave-lashed rocks below and the crew perished despite the frantic rescue attempts by Assistant Lightkeeper Wood. He later received the Queen's commendation for gallantry for his efforts.

During the automation work on the Bell Rock lighthouse there was one final drama when, on 3rd September 1987, a fire broke out in the tower. Fortunately there was no injury or loss of life and the lightkeepers were speedily evacuated in a well-coordinated rescue involving the R.N.L.I. and R.A.F. On 26th October 1988 the Bell Rock lighthouse, with its distinguishing character of one white flash every three seconds, was finally demanned and automated.

Off Fife Ness at the northern entrance to the Firth of Forth, there used to be moored the Northern Lighthouse Board's only manned lightvessel, marking the dangerous North Carr rock. The first lightvessel to be moored in this perilous position appeared on station in 1887 under the command of master mariner John Kirkpatrick. It was discovered that the North Carr lightvessel was moored in such an exposed position that after only four years on station completely new moorings had to be laid down. At the height of a November gale, despite a three ton anchor, the lightvessel drifted as far as a mile and a half off station. The original North Carr lightvessel was replaced by a more modern ship in 1933. Six years later with the onset of the Second World War, the lightvessel was removed to the less directly exposed waters of the Firth of Clyde. Back on station after the end of the war, all was quiet until one night in 1959 when the lightvessel broke her moorings in a severe gale and the seven man crew had to be rescued by helicopter. In 1975 the North Carr lightvessel was removed from service and replaced by a moored light buoy which was now backed up by the Northern lighthouse Board's newly constructed, unmanned, automatic lighthouse of Fife Ness. The old North Carr lightvessel became a floating museum in Anstruther harbour.

Now we come to the grandfather of them all. In the annals of Scottish lighthouse history, the Isle of May in the Firth of Forth is where it all began. As long ago as 1630 an enterprising chap called Alexander Cunningham of Barns petitioned King Charles the First for permission to erect a fire beacon on the Isle of May. King Charles referred the matter to the Scottish Privy Council and a Commission was set up to investigate the matter further. Giving evidence to the Commission, a Leith sea captain by the name of Thomas Lindsay stated that he reckoned that over £600,000 worth of ships and goods had been lost because the Isle of May was unlit. This, and other evidence

Isle of May lighthouse – where it all began.

received by the Commissioners persuaded them to grant Alexander Cunningham of Barns, and his son John, with a third partner named James Maxwell of Innerwick, permission to erect a lighthouse on the Isle of May. The terms set by the Commissioners were that the partners had to erect the lighthouse at their own expense, but all vessels sailing from the Forth beyond a line extending from Dunottar Castle to St. Abbs Head, or arriving in the Forth from outside these limits, were to pay two shillings (Scots) per ton if the ship was a Scottish one and four shillings (Scots) per ton if foreign. Out of this revenue the Crown was to receive £1,000 per annum. In 1636 the Isle of May lighthouse, consisting of a building twenty-five feet square with a vaulted roof, on top of which the coal-fired beacon burned, became Scotland's first manned operational lighthouse. Despite the formation of the Northern Lighthouse Board in 1786, the Isle of May lighthouse was to remain a private enterprise until it was finally taken over by them in 1814. In all those years the lighthouse had remained as a coal-fired beacon, a pretty unsatisfactory navigational aid which led to at least one disaster. This occurred in 1810 when the Royal Navy frigates *HMS Nymphe* and *HMS Pallas* (the famous 'fighting Pallas' of Captain Cochrane fame), were wrecked near Dunbar because the light of a lime kiln burning on the coast had been mistaken for the Isle of May lighthouse. The Northern Lighthouse Board Commissioners purchased the Isle of May along with the lighthouse and all interests in light dues, for the sum of £60,000, from the owners, the Duke and Duchess of Portland. Modernisation work began immediately, and by 1st February 1816 a new Isle of May lighthouse using oil-fired lamps for illumination, became operational.

Seventy years later the Isle of May lighthouse was to make history again when in a trial well ahead of its time, it became Scotland's first electrically-powered lighthouse. In June 1886 a carbon-arc light was installed but this early experiment in the use of electricity was far from being an overwhelming success and was to prove almost prohibitively expensive. Despite this, the Board were to persevere with it on the Isle of May for over thirty years before being finally forced to abandon the scheme and revert back to a paraffin light in 1924. By this time, the original generating equipment had become outdated and extremely unsafe to operate, and the maintenance costs were double those of any other lighthouse. A short time later another economy was made at the isle of May when the lighthouse station carthorse was taken off the island. This happened because someone pointed out that the only work the horse did was to cart its own fodder up from the landing! There was heroism at the Isle of May in 1930 when two of the keepers stationed at the lighthouse swam out to the Aberdeen trawler *George Aunger* which had been wrecked on the North Ness, and successfully rescued four fishermen. In 1972 the lightkeepers' families left the Isle of May for accommodation in Granton, Edinburgh, and the lighthouse was reclassified as an offshore rock lighthouse. Finally, on 31st March 1989, after 353 years, the lightkeepers finally left the Isle of May and the lighthouse was left to its own automated devices. The character of the Isle of May light consists of one white flash every twenty seconds.

Clinging seemingly precariously to the side of the distinctive bulk of the Bass Rock is the Bass Rock lighthouse established in 1902. This 60-foot high tower was constructed on the site of the castle in which Jacobite die-hard Charles Maitland held out for the deposed King James until August 1689. The lightkeepers on the Bass often used to find themselves playing host to visiting ornithologists who came to the island to study the gannet colonies. Seven per cent of all the gannets flying around in the world are hatched on this little rock, a fact celebrated in the bird's Latin name of *Sula bassana*. The Bass Rock is left to the gannets alone now as the lighthouse, with its character of six white flashes every thirty seconds, was demanned and made completely automatic in 1988.

Moving up the Firth of Forth we next call in on the little island of Fidra. The Northern Lighthouse Board established a lighthouse here in 1885 having, with some difficulty, acquired the land from the Dirleton estate. After the lighthouse had been built, the owners of the estate took the Board to court in an attempt to claim compensatory damage of £1,000 due to the inconvenience caused by the noise of the station's foghorn. They received little sympathy with their suit. Lord Justice Young, himself an ex-Commissioner, ironically enquired if the fog horn was more disagreeable than a quiet shipwreck! In 1970 the Fidra lighthouse was demanned and became the first major offshore lighthouse to become automatic and to be supervised by remote control.

Sitting plumb in the middle of the Firth of Forth with the city of Edinburgh to the south and Kinghorn and Kirkcaldy to the north on the Fife coast, is the small heavily fortified island of Inchkeith. Inchkeith lighthouse was built in 1804 on the site of an old castle which had been established by the order of Mary Queen of Scots. The establishment of a lighthouse here was partially instigated by the loss off Kinghorn of the smack, *Aberdeen,* from which there were only three survivors. Since the construction of Mary's castle in 1564, and most probably before that time too, this tiny island was of strategic military importance. In 1881 triple fortifications and gun batteries were constructed on the island with each battery able to bear its guns on any ship in the Firth of Forth. During both the First and Second World Wars the island was heavily garrisoned and further fortifications in the way of pillboxes and anti-aircraft emplacements were added. By the end of the 1960s the military had finally pulled out from the island abandoning their old barracks to be scavenged by succeeding Inchkeith lightkeepers. One chap I knew had an entire garden shed at his house ashore which was completely constructed from timber taken from the old army camp. When I worked at the lighthouse as a Supernumerary lightkeeper, a popular off-watch recreation was to go and play a game of snooker on the full-size table left behind in the derelict and abandoned NAAFI hut.

The lighthouse relief at Inchkeith, as for the other Forth lighthouses, was not usually accomplished by helicopter but by the tender, *Pharos*, which sailed from Granton. When I worked on the island the lightkeepers had come to an arrangement with the crews of the speedy Forth Pilot boats who kindly offered to take the newly-relieved keeper ashore. This saved him a long day aboard the *Pharos* as she did her rounds calling at the Isle of May, Bass Rock and Bell Rock. Inchkeith lighthouse once had its own boatman. The records report that back in 1890 the boatman was tragically drowned when his boat was swamped while being towed up the Forth by a tug.

The lighthouse on Inchkeith was far too much in the public eye for my liking. You had to be constantly on your guard, and while the quality of conscientiousness is a standard at any lighthouse, at Inchkeith you had to pay that little bit extra attention to duty as you never knew who might have their beady eyes trained on you through a pair of binoculars on the Edinburgh shore! Another problem was the fog horn which had to be switched off the exact instant that the visibility cleared otherwise headquarters would receive a spate of letters about the noise, signed 'Angry Fife Householder'! However, these problems are no more because Inchkeith lighthouse, one of the last paraffin lights with its distinguishing character of one white flash every fifteen seconds, was demanned and automated in 1986.

Not so far up the Forth from Inchkeith, is the 63-foot high tower of the Oxcars lighthouse which was constructed in 1886 and demanned just eight years later in 1894. The short life of the Oxcars lighthouse as a manned installation merits a mention for two reasons. The first of these is that this lighthouse was unusually and specifically designed as a two-man operated station, as opposed to the usual minimum of three at an offshore site.

There is an interesting and most probably apocryphal, story as to why offshore lighthouses are manned with a minimum of three men, which is well worth the telling. The tale goes that at a certain English offshore lighthouse many years ago, there were two lightkeepers who had just commenced their two month tour of duty when one of them dropped down dead! Of course, this was in the days long before radio and there was no way of signalling to the shore. The sole surviving lightkeeper was forced to wait until the relief boat came again with only the corpse of his former fellow keeper for company! He dared not dispose of the body in case he was accused of murder, and, as he was on a pillar rock lighthouse, there was nowhere to put it so it was always there in grim evidence. Apparently when the relief boat eventually arrived eight weeks later, they found the surviving keeper partially deranged and with his once raven black hair turned a snowy white! A good yarn to tell the tourists when they visit the lighthouse, you might say! But there may just be a kernel of truth in the tale. At all Scottish offshore lighthouses until quite recently, there used to be kept a small stock of wood which was specifically for the purpose of making a coffin should one of the lightkeepers die at the lighthouse. This was still the case not too many years ago when a pal of mine, who was quite keen on woodwork, found himself being reprimanded by the Principal lightkeeper after he had unwittingly constructed a rather tidy coffee table out of the lighthouse 'coffin wood'!

The second point of interest concerning the Oxcars lighthouse is that this was the very first Northern Lighthouse Board installation to be demanned and automated. In 1894 a gas burner was fitted, operated by a clockwork attachment which allowed the flame to burn for twenty-four hours but was only brought up to full power during the hours of darkness. Three gas holders were installed in the lighthouse which were filled once every fortnight from the Granton depot, the Oxcars lighthouse being quite easily reached at low tide. The system proved to be so successful and reliable that the men were taken off the Oxcars light for good, as previously mentioned, in 1896.

Oxcars is the last lighthouse in the Firth of Forth. The next of Scotland's south-east lighthouses, and the penultimate one on our farewell tour, is the one situated at Barns Ness near Dunbar. Barns Ness lighthouse was established in 1901 and is yet another Scottish lighthouse situated adjacent to a golf course. This also was another lighthouse which received unwelcome attention from enemy aircraft during World War Two, coming under attack only two weeks after the start of the hostilities. In 1966, it may well have been the first lighthouse in the world to be fitted with the advanced 'sealed beam' system of navigational light. This system consists not of a single lamp magnified by an optic but a series of sealed beam lamps, resembling car head lamps, usually numbering about nineteen in all and arranged in bands or tiers. At Barns Ness this new system produced an impressive maximum candle power of 1,300,000. Stroma lighthouse where I worked is fitted with the same system. From a lightkeeper's point of view it is an excellent setup which requires little attention. The only slight drawback with the sealed beam system is that the light must be exhibited up to half an hour before the official lighting-up time. This is in case one of the sealed beam units is defective. If this should be the case it can be quite a time-consuming operation to replace the defective lamp, as all the lamps have to be individually checked with an

Barns Ness lighthouse.

avometer to determine exactly which one has blown. The last lightkeeper at Barns Ness was Principal Duncan Jordan who, unusually at the time, was also the Principal lightkeeper at neighbouring St. Abbs Head lighthouse. This odd situation came about because Duncan's house at St. Abbs Head was being renovated, and as Barns Ness had been officially demanned in 1985, he and his family were temporarily accommodated in one of the empty dwelling houses there while he commuted back and forth for his watches at St. Abbs.

St. Abbs Head lighthouse is the final destination on our farewell tour of Scotland's lighthouses. The stubby tower of this lighthouse was first constructed in 1862 atop a 225-foot high cliff. This tiny lighthouse has the peculiarity of being situated at a lower level than the lightkeepers' dwelling houses, and must be one of the few where the lightkeeper on watch actually has to go downstairs to put the light in for the night. Being situated on such a high headland, and often subject to poor visibility, St. Abbs Head was the first Scottish lighthouse to be fitted with a fog siren, powered by hot air, in 1876. It was also the first to be fitted with a high-powered radio beacon in 1968. This shore-based lighthouse was, for a long time, an important communications centre being the radio control station in regular contact with the Firth of Forth lighthouses, as well as being the stand-by emergency contact when the Edinburgh headquarters were closed.

With the automation of all the Firth of Forth lighthouses, and the installation of the monitor centre manned twenty-four hours a day at headquarters in Edinburgh, St. Abbs Head lighthouse has now become something of a quiet backwater. When writing the first edition of the book, it was the only manned lighthouse left on the east coast of Scotland, but it was fully automated by 31st March 1994. The ten second-spaced white flashes now blink unattended. Like the rest of Scotland's lighthouses, the light will remain but the spark of life will be gone.

The control room at St Abbs Head in earlier days.

St Abbs light.

8

Life after the Light

Scotland's lighthouses have now all been de-manned. For well over a year now there have been no paraffin-oilers. The last to be de-manned was the lighthouse of Fair Isle South, the place which I nearly set on fire over twenty-five years ago.

On 31st March 1998 over 200 years of paraffin-oilers came to an end with a quiet ceremony attended by the Princess Royal. Angus Hutchinson, who had been the Principal at Fair Isle North during my involuntary arson escapade, was the last man out. An appropriate state of affairs as Angus was a true paraffin-oiler to the degree of four generations beginning with his great-grandfather back in the 1890s.

A month after this sad little episode on lonely Fair Isle, the Commissioners threw two parties, one in Edinburgh and one at Ackergill Tower in Caithness to which all us ex-lightkeepers were invited to show their appreciation for our years of service. Much whisky was drunk and if the Commissioners are still looking for their flag which mysteriously disappeared from the rugged battlements of Ackergill Tower, I did not pinch it ... but I know who did!

Because of the very nature of the job, I, and I suspect several of my old compatriots, have found it a hard act to follow. I had to leave the Service in 1994 and, since that time, I have worked as a car park attendant, did over two years further education which completely impoverished me and only taught me what a con the further education system can be, leaving me with multiple debts and qualifications which would probably help a young school leaver but were of little realistic use to a forty-something ex-lightkeeper. For eighteen months after that I worked in a call centre dispensing wisdom and assistance to the owners of mobile phones. While listening to Mr Angry from wherever bleating about his itemised call charges, my mind could not help but drift to days sitting watching the 'selkies' cavort in the landing inlet at Muckle Flugga on a summer's day. I have finally, though, found my niche as a local postie. Happy to be outdoors again and with the peace of mind once more to indulge in my pretensions to be a writer.

There are several ex-lightkeeper cronies living up here in the north. Some, like my two old pals Tommy Budge and Billy Gauld, happily accepted retirement. Sadly, Billy passed away early in 1999 and is sorely missed; I used to look forward to a pint with him in the Commercial bar in Thurso. Though even here there is some form of continuity with the lighthouses as Billy's son John is a fellow postie.

Among those of us too young for retirement, life after the light has sprung some variety. One old comrade is a local barman, another is in the roofing business and one has retrained and is now a male nurse. Alan Law, who was at Stroma lighthouse with me, was lecturing on photography for a while at the local college while working as the local boating pond attendant in the summer. Alan has just started work in the call centre which I happily left a year ago … bet he is back at the boating pond next summer.

The lighthouse stations themselves seem to have as much variety in life after the lightkeepers. I have heard that at least two are now upmarket guest houses under their new ownership.

Kinnaird Head has been transformed into the excellent Scottish Lighthouse Museum. Covesea and Point of Stoer are still providing holiday accommodation for ex-lightkeepers fancying a nostalgic holiday.

Several lighthouse stations merely transformed themselves into the private homes of the individuals who purchased the buildings from the Board. Dunnet Head was the focus of some notoriety a couple of years back when the present incumbent, a local pop star, was arrested by the local police for growing certain plants which I am sure never appeared on the Commissioners' list of recommended plants for lighthouse gardens.

Unfortunately all changes have not been for the better. I took a walk up to Holborn Head lighthouse at Scrabster a short time ago. I stayed here back in 1985 when Len Fraser was Principal and he kept the neat little station immaculate. The place has been uninhabited for a number of years now, and looks it. Local vandals have smashed the glass in all the lower windows which have now been boarded over. Paint is peeling and dirty and the access road is overgrown with weeds and liberally spattered with the offerings from the local canine population.

On the human side, I spoke to Jimmy Simpson the 'laird' of Stroma island. Sadly he said the place was just not the same without the keepers and that he would no longer go out to his island farm on his own in case he had an accident and be left helpless.

This last little sentence sums it up for me. There is life after the light, but let us pray that nobody is going to have an accident and be left helpless because there are now no more paraffin-oilers keeping a wary look out.

By the same author:

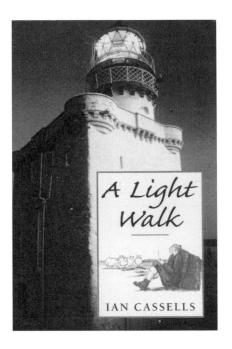

On duty in the cramped confines of Muckle Flugga Lighthouse, Ian Cassells walked circuits round the lighthouse station for exercise. In 1986 he went further and made a sponsored walk around all the manned lighthouses on the Scottish mainland. It took 58 days. Beautifully illustrated with 20 photographs and 24 specially-commissioned pen and ink drawings, *A Light Walk* is his light-hearted account of the 1100 mile walk.

Paperback 160pp   ISBN 1-870325-51-6

'...a perceptive eye for the beauty of the Highlands coupled with a nice sense of humour. A good read.'

'This book will delight many people and is thoroughly recommended.